"A wonderful book, full of encouragement for young girls everywhere."
—*Midwest Book Review*

"A useful self-help book and practical guide to life."
—*School Library Journal*

See
Jane
Win®

for Girls

—————•—————

A Smart Girl's
Guide to Success

See Jane Win®

for Girls

A Smart Girl's
Guide to Success

DR. SYLVIA RIMM

free spirit
PUBLISHING®

Works
for kids®

Library of Congress Cataloging-in-Publication Data
Rimm, Sylvia B., 1935–
　　See Jane win for girls : a smart girl's guide to success / Sylvia Rimm.
　　p. cm.
　　Summary: Presents tips, quizzes, activities, and words of wisdom from successful women for girls trying to make positive changes and choices in all areas of their lives and develop confidence, inner strength, and the desire to learn.
　　Includes bibliographical references and index.
　　ISBN 1-57542-122-4
　　1. Teenage girls—Psychology—Juvenile literature. 2. Girls—Psychology—Juvenile literature. 3. Self-perception in adolescence—Juvenile literature. 4. Self-esteem in adolescence—Juvenile literature. 5. Success—Psychological aspects—Juvenile literature. 6. Achievement motivation in women—Juvenile literature. [1. Conduct of life. 2. Self-esteem. 3. Self-perception. 4. Success.] I. Title.

HQ798.R56 2003
305.235—dc21
2002155780

Edited by Jacqueline Glasthal
Cover and interior design by Marieka Heinlen
Illustrations by Chris Sharp
Photos from Artville Stock Images
Index by Randl Ockey

10 9 8 7 6 5 4 3 2
Printed in the United States of America

Free Spirit Publishing Inc.
217 Fifth Avenue North, Suite 200
Minneapolis, MN 55401-1299
(612) 338-2068
help4kids@freespirit.com
www.freespirit.com

The following are registered trademarks of Free Spirit Publishing Inc.:

FREE SPIRIT®
FREE SPIRIT PUBLISHING®
THE FREE SPIRITED CLASSROOM®
SELF-HELP FOR KIDS®
SELF-HELP FOR TEENS®
WORKS FOR KIDS®
HOW RUDE!™
LEARNING TO GET ALONG™
LAUGH & LEARN™

Dedication

To my children and grandchildren whose names are scattered throughout the book. It's fun to see our granddaughters raised to be smart, hardworking, kind, and independent girls, and our grandsons raised to not only be smart, hardworking, kind, and independent, but also to respect and value strong and smart girls.

Acknowledgments

I want to thank many wonderful people who help me advise girls on how to grow up successful and happy. First, I'd like to acknowledge with great appreciation the more than 1,000 successful *See Jane Win* and *How Jane Won* women who shared their stories and their wise advice. They help me inspire girls to fulfill themselves.

A special thank you extends to my editor Jackie Glasthal who assisted me in creatively adapting and organizing the *See Jane Win* research to interest, encourage, and excite young girls. I also appreciate my publisher Judy Galbraith who, together with her staff, carefully reviewed and published the book so it would be available to everyone who made *See Jane Win* a *New York Time*s best-selling success.

Finally, I appreciate my patient and willing staff, Marilyn Knackert, Joanne Riedl, and Karen Block, who assisted me in readying my book for publication. As always, I extend great appreciation to my agent, Pierre Lehu, who assists and encourages me with all my publications.

I also have a special thank you for my grandchildren, Rachel Rimm, Hannah Rimm, Daniel Rimm, and Benjamin Rimm Madsen. They read the book in its early stages to help me determine its readability for tweens. Special thanks also go to some *See Jane Win* women and their girls who provided early reviews. They included Camellia Okpodu and her daughters Samelia, Elizabeth, and Koren; Elaine Kraut and her granddaughter Lindsey; Janet Schiller and her daughter Hannah; and Teresa Culver and her daughter Sarah.

Contents

Introduction

Welcome, Readers!

Maybe you feel ordinary or extraordinary. Maybe you enjoy basketball, hanging with your friends at the mall, or lying in the sun with a good book. Maybe you know what you'd like to do when you grow up or maybe you don't. But you're someone with plenty of potential. Want to make the most of it? Then keep reading!

See Jane Win for Girls is loaded with tips, quizzes, activities, and words of wisdom that grew out of a study I did with over 1,000 successful women. I asked them to describe how they felt and what they did when they were kids, and how those experiences helped them to become the grown-ups they are. Using what we learned from this study, my daughters and I wrote two books for adults, *See Jane*

Win and *How Jane Won.* Today those books are helping many people raise their daughters to be the best they can be.

Now, in *See Jane Win for Girls* I bring some of these stories, lessons, and memories to you directly. You'll find that when they were girls, many *See Jane Win* women thought of themselves as pretty ordinary, maybe even boring. Some felt (and were told by friends or grown-ups) that they were too serious, too silly, too bossy, too shy, too lonely, too mean, too nice, too pretty, too ugly, too smart, or not smart enough. Yet they all developed confidence, inner strength, and the desire to learn—what many adults call a healthy self-esteem. (You'll read more about this in chapter 2.) Their experiences also helped them become what in this book I refer to as I CAN girls. (See pages 4–7 for more on what that means.)

Some Things You Should Know Before You Get Started

Throughout *See Jane Win for Girls* you'll find circles labeled "And the Survey Says," which highlight information from my study that I think you'll find interesting. I've included lots of quotes from the women I interviewed. These are in boxes. Some of the women asked me not to use their real names. When you see an * beside a name, the name has been made up, but the story belongs to a real person. For a summary of each chapter's major points, check out the "I CAN: Tips for How You Can" at the end of each chapter.

I wrote *See Jane Win for Girls* for all kinds of girls living in all kinds of family situations. So not every word will apply exactly to you and your family. I may talk about a brother when you have a sister, or a stepmother when you have a grandfather, an aunt, or a mother. But no matter what your situation, a lot of the advice will apply to your own life.

Remember:

Families come in many forms. The word "parents," as it's used here, refers to the adults at home who are responsible for you. And "sisters" and "brothers" are the other kids who live with you. Even if the people you live with aren't actually related to you, you still can consider them your family.

How to Use This Book

You may want to read *See Jane Win for Girls* on your own, but it might be even better to read it with a friend, teacher, parent, grandparent, cousin, sister, or even brother. Reading it with another person might lend her to tell you some interesting stories about herself. You may find out that you have more in common with Aunt Ethel or Uncle C.J. than you ever would have imagined. After all, times change, but feelings like shyness, anger, loneliness, love, loss, insecurity, and uncertainty don't.

Reading the book together will also give you a chance to ask questions that you otherwise might not get a chance to ask, and it will give the other person a chance to ask you questions. What kinds of questions? Check out the "Discussion Guide: Digging Deeper" section at the back of this book (see pages 120–124).

And speaking of questions—let me know if you have any for me. To write me, just visit my *www.seejanewin.com* Web site, and click on email. I'll do my best to get back to you as soon as I can.

Keep reading . . . and stay in touch!
Your friend,

Sylvia Rimm

Chapter 1

Dare to Dream

Do you ever wonder what your future will be like? Do you think you might grow up to be a marine biologist, a veterinarian, a fourth-grade teacher, an adventurer, or a television star? Maybe you're thinking you'd like to get married and have kids and live in an apartment in a large city or in a house in the country. Or maybe you secretly dream of becoming the first woman president of the United States.

Why not? You can have a bright future, and daring to dream is part of creating it. But dreaming isn't enough. For dreams to come true, you have to take action, too. That means becoming an I CAN girl. This book will tell you how.

Anything's Possible!

Many of today's successful women dreamed of doing something special when they were your age. Janice Huff, the meteorologist on NBC's *Weekend Today* knew she wanted to study weather by the time she was in kindergarten. She and her grandpa used to sit on the porch of their home in South Carolina and watch the storms roll in. By third or fourth grade, she was studying maps in encyclopedias, and when she discovered that people who predicted the weather were called meteorologists, she knew that was what she wanted to be when she grew up.

Catherine Burns* wanted to be a first-grade teacher in first grade, a second-grade teacher in second grade, a third-grade teacher in third grade, and . . . well, you get the picture. When she finally went to the Massachusetts Institute of Technology as a graduate student after four years of college, she thought she'd like to be a

professor there, and eventually that's what she did. She changed her mind many times along the way about what she wanted to teach. But she never stopped dreaming about standing in front of a classroom.

Some successful women didn't know as kids what they wanted to be. NASA astronaut and space shuttle commander Eileen Collins was one of them. She was a shy girl who got average grades in school, she says. But she became passionate about astronomy one summer at camp as she stared up at the stars. She began thinking about a profession where she could see them up close when she became an adult.

Television news anchor Donna Draves* didn't have a career picked out as a child either. But she did want to do something special. Now she has a career she loves and feels that she has fulfilled her childhood dream.

Your future is something to imagine, to think about, and even to plan for. But don't panic if you don't already know exactly what you want to do when you grow up. This is a great time to discover your skills and talents, and to develop them. That's what television news anchor Jane Pauley and Massachusetts district attorney Martha Coakley did. Both were active in speech and debate when they were younger. This led them to careers where speaking skills count. Your interests can lead you to something you'll enjoy doing for the rest of your life, too!

Are You an I CAN Girl?

Many of the women you'll read about in *See Jane Win for Girls* were I CAN girls when they were growing up. That means that they loved to take on new challenges and become actively involved in things that interested them. They brought a positive attitude to much of what they did. Some of them tried their best from the start. Others—like attorney Martha Lindner—had to learn to do that. Martha still remembers how auditioning for a solo singing part in fourth grade changed

her. She was a shy child and sang timidly while her friend, who was also auditioning, belted out her song. Martha was disappointed when her friend got the solo. But the experience taught her that if she didn't take the risk of doing her best, she'd lose her chance. Martha made up her mind to be an I CAN girl, even though it meant getting laughed at if she messed up.

In your grandmother's day, women were often laughed at if they dreamed of becoming anything other than a mother, a nurse, or a teacher. Luckily, those days are gone. Today you can do the kinds of things that women have traditionally done or you can do things that have traditionally been done by men. You may want to do something ordinary or extraordinary. Either way, you can begin thinking and preparing now. Sure, some people may not think much of your dreams and ambitions. Yours are bound to be different from those of other people you know. And don't be surprised if your goals change as you get older. Suzanne Daniels*, a state senator, never guessed as a child that one day she'd see her name on an election ballot. She always thought she'd be a homemaker and science teacher. Other successful women had several careers before settling into one that felt right.

No matter what you decide to do in life, though, you'll have to be determined and creative. That's what being an I CAN girl is all about.

> *It never dawned on me that, because I was a black kid growing up during the worst period of racism in Alabama, I was inferior to anyone. I never believed the word can't. It's a word I don't use. Everything I've done in my life I've been told I couldn't do, so when someone tells me what I can't do, I know I'm on the right track.*
>
> **–Marva Collins, Founder, Marva Collins Preparatory School, Chicago**

QUICK QUIZ

Are You on the Path to Your Dreams?
Where are you on the road to becoming an I CAN girl? Take the quiz on the next page to find out. Write your answers on a separate sheet of paper. That way you can take the quiz again another time, or invite a friend to take it. When you're done, you may want to talk about your answers with important people in your life. But don't compare your answers with anyone else's to see who did "better." There are no winners or losers here. The quiz is meant to help you and your friends become the best you can be so you all can achieve your goals.

1. **Write the number that best describes what you think about your future.**

   1 - I can't imagine that I'll ever do anything important or really cool.

   3 - I expect that when I grow up I'll have an important job and cool hobbies.

   2 - I may grow up to do something important, but it's hard to imagine.

2. Count the adults you can think of (mom, dad, grandmother, grandfather, aunt, uncle, teacher, and so on) who have told you they think you might do something special when you grow up. **Write that number on your paper.**

   1   2   3   4+

3. **Write the number that best describes how smart you feel.**

   4 - Really smart

   2 - A little below average

   3 - Average

   1 - Don't ask

4. **Write the number that best describes how much you like to read.**

   1 - Not much

   4 - A lot

   3 - Pretty much

   2 - A little

5. **Write the number of activities and lessons you take outside of school.**

   0   1   2   3   4+

6. **Write the number that best describes how you deal with competition.**

   2 - I hate to lose. It makes me mad or sad, and sometimes I quit.

   1 - I hate competition and stay away unless I'm sure I can win.

   4 - I love competition and keep trying, even when I lose.

7. **Write the number that best describes how much you speak up in school.**

   2 - I volunteer to speak up once in a while.

   4 - I speak up a lot in class.

   3 - I speak up an average amount.

   1 - I don't ever speak up unless I'm called on.

8. **Write the number that best describes how independent you are.**

   2 - I don't like doing things alone but will sometimes if no one else is around.

   4 - I like thinking up things to do on my own sometimes.

   1 - I only do things with friends, never alone.

9. **Write the number that best describes how hard a worker you are.**

   1 - I don't like hard work and try not to.

   4 - I work very hard and stay with it, even when things are difficult.

   3 - I work pretty hard but sometimes give up when the work is too tough.

10. **Write the number that best describes how you think.**

    4 - I have a lot of good ideas.

    2 - I hardly ever have good ideas.

    1 - I never have any good ideas.

    3 - Sometimes I have good ideas.

11. **Write the number that best describes your friends.**

    3 - Most of my friends are good students.

    2 - Some of my friends are good students and some are not.

    1 - Most of my friends are not good students.

12. **Write the number that best describes how you feel about the advice you get from adults.**

    1 - The adults I know don't understand me, so I often ignore what they say.

    2 - Even when adults give me good advice, sometimes I'd rather not take it.

    4 - I'm lucky to know adults I can turn to for advice when I have a problem.

WHAT'S YOUR SCORE?

If you've been honest with yourself, you've probably answered some questions on this quiz with 1s, or 2s and others with 3s or 4s. The 3s and 4s are your strengths and the 1s are your weaknesses. (The 2s are somewhere in the middle.) Add up all your scores. If the total is:

30 or above You have a bright future ahead. Reading this book will encourage you and give you confidence to follow your dreams.

15–29 You may hit a few roadblocks on your way. This book will help you get back on track toward your dreams.

14 or below It's time to make some changes so you can dare to dream. This book will help point you in the right direction.

The goal here isn't to have a perfect score. It's to believe in yourself and your ability to learn as you grow. Remember that you can learn from mistakes and that if you don't make some mistakes, you're probably not learning.

My athletic coaches taught me much more about life than about sports. In high school, my gymnastics coach did not want to put me on the team because she said I was not trying hard enough. She said, "You can't give halfway; you've got to give everything you have, and you will do wonderfully." She was right. I did very well in competitions after that, but it took hard work.

–Catherine Calloway, CNN Headline News Anchor

Follow Your Heart and Your Head

Maybe you were born in America or maybe you were born in Mexico, Laos, Canada, Japan, India, Russia, Somalia, or Iran. Maybe your parents, grandparents, or great-grandparents were immigrants, as my parents were. No matter what they do or where they came from, the adults who are raising you probably have worked hard and made sacrifices so that you can have a good education and other opportunities. That's something grown-ups often want to do for the young people in their life.

If you'd like, ask a parent or another adult you know what their dreams were when they were your age. Which ones did they achieve? Do they have dreams they're still pursuing? How did their dreams change along the way?

But always remember: Their dreams don't have to be your dreams. You can choose to follow in their footsteps or you can follow your own dream. That's what's so exciting: The choice is entirely up to you!

I grew up very poor in a rural town in Puerto Rico. My father worked in the sugarcane fields. Neither of my parents was formally educated, but they instilled in me the value of learning. Every morning my father reminded us that education was the only way out of the cycle of poverty. Poverty challenged me to excel, to go to college, to become a professional, and to be able to provide for my family.

–Nydia Velázquez, U.S. Congresswoman from New York

My grandparents literally walked across Europe to come to this country. If they hadn't escaped when they did, neither side of my family would have survived the Second World War. They came to America with absolutely no money or possessions. My parents were not well educated, but education was important in our home because that was the way to live the American Dream. My dad was a waiter, but my parents were able to put their daughters through college. It was wonderful to become a congresswoman so I could give something back to my country.

–Shelley Berkley, U.S. Congresswoman from Nevada

I CAN!

Tips for How You Can
Learn to Follow Your Dreams

- Know that it's never too early to imagine, think about, and plan for your future.

- Participate fully in everything that you do. Take the risk of making your best effort!

- Don't be afraid to take on new challenges.

- Don't give up—*especially* when things get tough! Avoid using words like *can't* or *impossible.*

- Believe in yourself and in your ability to learn as you grow.

- Trust that you can find interests that are right for you.

Chapter 2

Exercising Your Self-Esteem Muscles

Odd as it may sound, your self-esteem—how you feel about yourself—can help shape your future. When you respect yourself and your values, feel good about what you've achieved, and have confidence in your abilities, your self-esteem is healthy. People usually call this good self-esteem. Good self-esteem lets you tackle new challenges and take the risks that go along with being creative, independent, and strong. These are important steps that can also lead you to do much more when you're an adult.

If you're an I CAN girl with good self-esteem, you know you can do wonderful things. And when you make a mistake—which is bound to happen—you don't let it drag you down. You understand that no one is perfect, and that setbacks can still lead to successes. As long as you learn from your mistakes and keep growing, your failures will only be temporary. With an outlook like this, you can have courage to make choices that are right for you.

When I catch myself worrying, I make myself sit down and write affirmations that I put by my dresser. I look at them in the morning before I go to work: "I'm good at what I do." "I have support for my direction." "I can reach out to others." When I write down these affirmations, I feel like I'm digging inside myself to get on the right track. These help me focus on dealing positively with the issues.

I also use imagery to see myself being successful. I learned the technique at a leadership conference at an outdoor learning center. We had to climb on high ropes. I hate heights and was really scared and shaking, so I visualized myself jumping across the ropes like a squirrel, and enjoying it. It worked. I completed the ropes course without falling. I felt really proud I had conquered a fear. When I see myself succeed, I do.

—Charlotte Otto, Senior Vice-President and Global External Relations Officer, Procter & Gamble

Evaluating Your Self-Esteem

All kids lose confidence in a skill or ability once in a while. When this happens to you, it doesn't mean you have low self-esteem. It just means you know that you're not as good at some things as you'd like to be, or as you are at others. You may wish you could be voted Class Brain, Most Popular, or Best Athlete. But as long as you remember that most kids aren't any of these things, you don't have to feel bad about it. You have choices: You can shrug your shoulders and remember that you have your strengths and other kids have theirs. Or you can resolve to work on getting better in the areas that really matter to you. Either way, remember that if you set your mind

to it and make a real effort, you can develop your skills.

Your self-esteem is low when you feel bad about most things. For example, if you see yourself as a poor student with no special abilities, as someone nobody likes, or as someone who can't get along with anyone, that's a problem. When that happens, it's important to affirm yourself (as Charlotte Otto did) and learn to appreciate yourself for who you are. Affirming yourself means finding your best qualities and using them to help you feel positive about yourself as a whole.

Part of growing up is learning to accept yourself and face your problems. But figuring out which issues to focus on—what to improve and what to accept as it is—takes a lot of thought and a lot of soul searching. Just remember that everyone has both strengths and weaknesses and that self-respect and self-esteem are the keys to being an I CAN girl—a good and positive person who's enthusiastic about learning and growing.

Creating a Strengths, Weaknesses, and Changes Chart

The first step toward accepting your strengths and weaknesses is to figure out what they are. (That makes sense, doesn't it?) Here is a list of characteristics that the *See Jane Win* women used when describing themselves as kids. As you look over the list, think about which characteristics apply to you. Of these, which are you happy about and which do you wish you didn't have?

How Many of these Characteristics Apply to You?

adult-like	mean
athletic	modest
beautiful	nerdy
bossy	perfectionistic
book loving	persistent
brainy	popular
cool	princess-like
courageous	quiet
confident	rebellious
creative	risk taking
different	sad
emotional	secure
fashionable	self-critical
fearful	sensitive
follower	shy
funny	smart
gifted	special
good	strong willed
happy	sweet
hard working	talented
immature	talkative
independent	tomboyish
kind	troublemaking
lazy	unhappy
leading	very social
lonely	wimpy

Using these words, and any others that describe you well, create a **Strengths, Weaknesses, and Changes Chart,** like the ones Khana and Laura made (see page 13). Here's how:

1. Make a photocopy of the chart on page 14. Or, if you want more space to write, copy it onto a larger blank sheet of paper.

2. **Strengths.** In the first column, list your skills and abilities and the personality traits and aspects of your appearance that you like. (Don't forget to refer to the list of characteristics to the left for ideas.)

3. **Things to Improve.** In the second column, list areas you'd like to work on.

4. **Changes to Make.** In the third column, list changes you could make that would help you feel even better about yourself. But be realistic. Some things (like height, skin color, disabilities, or living situation) are very difficult or impossible to change or control.

5. **Things to Accept.** List the things that are out of your control—the ones you'll have to learn to live with—in the fourth column of the chart.

As you continue reading *See Jane Win for Girls,* you'll probably get some new ideas about how to deal with the things you'd like to improve—and about how to accept the things you can't change. When that happens, come back and add them to your chart if you want to.

Khana's Strengths, Weaknesses, and Changes Chart

Strengths	Things to Improve	Changes to Make	Things to Accept
GOOD WRITER	AVERAGE IN SCIENCE	ASK MANUELA, WHO IS GOOD AT SCIENCE, TO STUDY WITH ME FOR OUR WEEKLY QUIZZES.	MY HEIGHT (WISH I WAS TALLER)
GOOD READER	AVERAGE IN MATH		HOW SOFT MY VOICE IS.
FRIENDLY	SOMETIMES FORGET CHORES	STOP DOING MATH HOMEWORK IN FRONT OF THE TV!	MY CURLY HAIR
GOOD HELPER	STUBBORN		
PERSISTENT	A LITTLE SHY	CREATE A SCHEDULE SHOWING WHEN I HAVE CHORES TO DO.	
UNDERSTANDING OF FRIENDS			
LEADER WITH SOME FRIENDS		ACCEPT THAT IT'S OKAY TO CHANGE MY MIND SOMETIMES.	
LIKES SCHOOL			
CREATIVE THINKER		SPEAK UP MORE IN CLASS. COULD ALSO AUDITION FOR THE SCHOOL PLAY, OR JOIN THE DEBATE CLUB FOR PRACTICE TALKING IN FRONT OF OTHERS.	
KIND PERSON			
GOOD BIG SISTER			
PRETTY NICE LOOKING			
GOOD COORDINATION FOR SPORTS			

Laura's Strengths, Weaknesses, and Changes Chart

Strengths	Things to Improve	Changes to Make	Things to Accept
GOOD SINGING VOICE	BAD STUDENT	ASK TO GET A TUTOR	DIABETES
GOOD LISTENER	LONELY A LOT	JOIN THE CHURCH CHOIR.	THAT MY SISTER AND I HAVE TO SHARE A ROOM
GOOD AT ART	MEAN TO MY SISTER	BE NICE TO MY SISTER	
	LOSE MY TEMPER	COUNT TO 10 AND TAKE DEEP BREATHS WHEN I FEEL MYSELF GETTING ANGRY	MY FRECKLES
	BOYS DON'T LIKE ME		
	GIRLS LEAVE ME OUT		
	TOO FAT	EAT LESS JUNK FOOD AND EXERCISE MORE	
	BAD AT SPORTS	FIND A SPORT I LIKE	

My Own Strengths, Weaknesses, and Changes Chart

Strengths	Things to Improve	Changes to Make	Things to Accept

Getting a Handle on Your Strengths and Weaknesses

Take a moment to compare Khana and Laura's Strengths, Weaknesses, and Changes Charts. You'll see that Khana's list of strengths is her longest list, while Laura's is very short. And Laura's second and third lists are longer than Khana's are. That means there are more things about herself that Laura wishes she could change. Since it would be very difficult, if not impossible, for her to change so many things about herself—especially all at once—Laura will probably just feel worse the more she tries.

If she takes a closer look at the things she'd like to improve, though, Laura may notice that some things can be grouped together. For example, losing her temper, acting mean, feeling lonely, and being disliked by other kids are all related to her social skills. If she didn't lose her temper and act mean, she'd probably have an easier time making friends and wouldn't feel so lonely. By grouping them together, and seeing the connections, Laura gets a shorter list of improvements to focus on. She also sees some things she can do about her problems. (Social skills are covered in chapter 4.)

Laura can also ask herself if she's being too hard on herself. For example, she writes that she's a "bad student." But what does that really mean? Is she failing every subject? Or does she consider anything short of straight A's a failure? Would her grades be better if she handed in her homework on time? Does she need to work on her test-taking skills? Should she focus on a few subjects a bit more or get help with them?

Instead of putting herself down by calling herself a bad student, Laura can try to pinpoint the areas she needs to work on. Then, if she needs to, she can talk to a parent, teacher, or guidance counselor about how to get the help she needs.

Now look at Khana's chart. In making her lists, she found that one of her strengths (persistence) and an area in which she needs improvement (stubbornness) are related! Persistence means that Khana doesn't give up easily. But her stubbornness, which she sees as a problem, actually helps her persist. She will have to work hard to figure out when she's being stubborn and when she's being persistent.

Turn to your lists now. Do you see anything that can be grouped together? Are you being too hard on yourself? Do you have strengths with a downside or problem areas with an upside? If so, how does seeing the two sides make you feel different about your pluses and minuses? Can you use your strengths to help yourself in areas where you're weak?

As you examine your Strengths, Weaknesses, and Changes Chart, use questions like these to help you look at your problem areas in a new way. Then read on to see if you recognize yourself in some of the self-esteem issues in the rest of the chapter.

> *The advice I give all kids, especially young black women, is to always be your best. It's not just because you think someone is watching, but be your best, keep yourself sharp, so no one can ever pass you over and say you're not qualified.*
>
> **–Deborah Roberts, Correspondent, ABC's 20/20 Newsmagazine**

Is Perfectionism a Problem for You?

Trying to do your best in everything from science to band, from soccer to keeping your room neat, is usually a good thing. It's part of what being an I CAN girl is all about. But if you feel that nothing you do is ever good enough, or that anything short of perfection makes you a failure, you're being way too hard on yourself. That's because doing your best (which is possible) is different from being perfect (which is not).

When she was a girl learning the violin, professional musician Pamela Frank remembers getting upset whenever she didn't play perfectly. When she was about eight, she hit a wrong note while performing for her grandparents and ran to her bedroom to sulk.

"So who do you think you are, the famous violinist Itzhak Perlman?" her parents teased her. They were making a joke, but they were also telling her to lighten up a bit. Pamela learned to laugh at her mistakes, and also to learn from them.

What about you? Are you a perfectionist? Ask yourself the following questions to find out. Don't give what you think are the right answers. Give the answers that are most often true for you.

1. Do you worry that most of what you do is not good enough?

2. Do you often criticize yourself?

3. Do you get upset when someone criticizes something you've done?

4. Are you afraid to try new things because you might not succeed?

5. Do you lie in bed at night worrying about a mistake you made that day or a B you got on a test?

6. Do you drop out of activities because you're not the best at them?

7. Do you have a hard time starting projects because no topic feels quite right?

8. Do you study more than any other kid you know?

If you've answered yes to some of these questions, you may be a bit of a perfectionist. Here are some things you can try:

• Take pride in your efforts. When you've completed a project that you've worked hard on, give yourself credit for what you have done.

• Learn to see your mistakes and other people's criticism as proof that you're challenging yourself. Tell yourself, "I made a mistake, but that's okay. What lessons can I learn from this?"

• If you're studying more than anyone else in your class, try cutting back your study time by ten minutes a day. If it doesn't lower your grade, cut your study time ten minutes more until you find the right balance between study time and good grades. If your grades go down while you're experimenting, add back some study time. Be proud of your good study habits, but leave yourself time for fun, too!

• Enter a contest or try an activity that you may not be very good at. Take a chance! Don't even think about being the best. Record your progress as you go along, and compare it to where you started. For example, if you try running, keep track of how much your speed or distance improves. If you try music, play an easy song every so often and remember how hard it once was.

Dance taught me a huge amount of discipline. If I didn't workout properly, if I didn't rehearse, if I stayed out too late, or if I ate too much, I felt it the next day. When I came out of dance and applied what I learned to other fields, I knew how to work hard. But dance also increased my tendency to be a perfectionist, to make everything a more painful ordeal than it has to be. With perfectionism, the end is what's important and not the process. Who knows? Maybe I would still have arrived where I am if I'd been more relaxed and open to other possibilities. But because of my perfectionism, risks take a lot out of me.

—**Janet Schiller, Television News Producer, NBC's TODAY**

- Read stories about successful women. Notice how many times they learned from their failures and mistakes, and how they coped with hard times.

- Compliment a friend, sister, or brother about something they've done—especially something that you wish you could do. You'll be amazed how good it feels to help someone else feel good about their strengths, and it will help you accept that you don't have to be the best at everything.

- Ask a parent or teacher to make written suggestions about how you can improve a project. Thank her for the ideas. Then decide which pieces of advice (if any) you want to take. Remind yourself that it's okay to have different opinions, and the suggestions were meant to help you, not criticize you.

- When you need a topic for an essay, a research report, or a science project, quickly jot down as many ideas as you can. Don't criticize any of them until you have a long list. Then whittle down the ideas until you're left with the ones you feel are the best.

- If, like Pamela, you see yourself becoming too serious about things sometimes, take a tip from Pamela's parents: Try laughing at your own mistakes.

An I CAN Girl Doesn't Have to Be Perfect

On swim team, I try my hardest to learn the strokes exactly the way my coach shows them to me. She usually praises me for my perfectionism and tells me it will help me become an expert swimmer. My swim team members don't mind because a few of them seem perfectionistic, too.

In school, I'm in the gifted program and I work hard to complete my projects perfectly. I usually get A+s, and my teacher's comments often include the word "perfect." Once in a while, some of the other kids make fun of my need to be so perfect, but that doesn't bother me much. I feel proud of my schoolwork.

At home, I have a big problem. I share my room with my sister, and her part of the room is a mess. Her sloppiness totally bothers me. When I ask her to clean up, she calls me a perfectionist and gets really angry. I think she resents my neatness. When my mom asks her to clean her clutter, she blames that on my perfectionism, too.

I've been thinking about the pluses and minuses of my perfectionism. I enjoy doing excellent work, and when others around me are pleased with my work it makes me feel proud. But it's when I make someone else look bad by comparison or get them into trouble because they're not as good at something as I am, they seem angry at me. I don't mean to make them feel bad but I just have to set my goals high. I decided I should sort out what really needs to be perfect and where I can be a little more relaxed. Maybe I could be a little easier on my sister about our room and she wouldn't get into so much trouble with Mom. It will be hard for me to ease up, but I'm going to try. A perfectly neat room isn't as important as excellent schoolwork, and maybe I'll even feel more relaxed when she and I get along better.—Kayla

If Your Self-Esteem Depends on What Others Think of You

Everyone needs support from friends, relatives, and teachers. Important people in our lives make a difference in how we feel about ourselves. But sometimes kids (and even adults) worry more about pleasing others than they do about pleasing themselves. When this happens, criticism is especially hard to take.

If you're too concerned about what others think of you, you may be waiting for these people to boost your self-esteem for you. But no one can please everyone all the time. Parents can't, teachers can't, your friends can't, the most popular kids in your school can't—not even rock stars or athletes or powerful leaders can please everyone all the time! After all, do you *always* like the way your friends dress? Do you agree with *everything* your parents or teachers say? Are you *ever* critical of others—in your head, if not out loud? Disagreements are healthy and normal. They're bound to happen. That's because everyone has an individual point of view—including you! If you tend to be friendly, kind, and caring, you should be able to feel good about yourself just as you are, even if it's not the way others want you to be. And if you do feel good about yourself, chances are you'll make friends who feel good about you, too.

So be your own best friend. And give yourself a break. Once you accept yourself as a worthy person, you may not feel as bad if someone doesn't sit with you in the cafeteria or invite you to her party. You'll also be less likely to go along with a crowd if they're leading you someplace you'd rather not go. And it will be much easier to accept criticism gracefully, or even shrug off rude remarks if you know that, no matter what anyone else says, you're doing your best and you're growing and improving every single day!

> *At the end of the day, you're the one making decisions if you're in a leadership position. You have to have the ability to analyze and believe in your decisions, and then stand by them. You can't define yourself in terms of others.*
> **—Christine Todd Whitman, Administrator, U.S. Environmental Protection Agency; former governor of New Jersey**

Instead of being crushed by criticism, remind yourself that no one is perfect and that you don't have to please everyone. Then ask yourself these questions to help identify your critic's motives:

- Was this criticism meant to help or hurt me?

- Is there anything that I can learn from it?

- Should I change the way I've done something?

- Should I ignore this criticism?

- Should I tell the person who was critical of me how these comments made me feel?

If you decide that someone's comments were mean spirited, and maybe not even true, you may want to ignore them—especially if they came from a kid who often bullies others and says cruel things. Unless you're being harassed and feel that you may be in danger (in which case you should tell a parent, teacher, or other adult right away), try not to let that kid's opinions matter to you.

But if the comments came from someone who you care about—like a parent or a true friend—think hard about what that person was trying to tell you. Is there anything you can learn from it? After all, real friends don't usually say hurtful things to each other on purpose. Neither do parents or others who truly care about you. So look at yourself honestly and figure out what the person was objecting to. Then decide whether you agree.

> *My experience as an African-American girl helped me immeasurably as a woman. Because I had experienced rejection, I learned every day not to count on others' acceptance as a measure of my worth.*
>
> **—Dr. Alexa Canady, Neurosurgeon**

IT DOESN'T SEEM FAIR TO ME THAT YOU CALL ME LAZY WHEN I FORGET ONCE IN A WHILE. IT SEEMS LIKE YOU WANT ME TO BE PERFECT AND THAT MAKES ME REALLY SAD. CAN WE TALK ABOUT THIS LATER? I WISH YOU DIDN'T HAVE TO GET SO MAD AT ME WHEN I MAKE A MISTAKE ONCE IN A WHILE.

LOVE, CARRIE

Even if you decide that a person's criticism had some truth in it, negative statements (like "Have you thought about going on a diet?" "Stop being so bossy!" or "This room is a disaster area!") don't have to leave you feeling horrible about yourself. If they do, though, talk to yourself about it. You might tell yourself, "My friend doesn't have to like my new hairstyle. But I still need to decide what I think. I'll give myself a few days to get used to it. Then I'll figure out what to do." Or, "My mom was really mad when I didn't take out the garbage. I know she's been pretty stressed lately so I'll try not to take her tone of voice too personally."

If that doesn't help enough, wait until you've calmed down a bit. Then tell the person how his or her statements left you feeling. Or if that's too hard, try writing a note instead:

DEAR DADDY,
YOU KNOW I LOVE YOU SO MUCH BUT I HATED IT WHEN YOU CALLED ME LAZY THE OTHER DAY. I'M SORRY I DIDN'T FEED THE DOG ON TIME, BUT I DID DO IT RIGHT AFTERWARDS.

Your dad or mom may still get mad if you forget to do your chores. A close friend may still say you're too bossy sometimes, or that she doesn't like the other kids you hang around with. But hopefully, if you explain how hurtful their comments can be, these people will be more respectful of your feelings and more careful about how they put their comments. (If this doesn't work, or if someone *only* has negative things to say to you, no matter what you've done well or how hard you've tried, it's time to get help from a grown-up you trust.)

Remember: You can feel smart without having to be smartest. You can have friends without having to be most popular. And you can be athletic, musical, or artistic without having to be the best. If you'd like, tape a note to your mirror that says, "I don't have to be perfect or be liked by everyone to feel good about myself. I am an I CAN girl!"

> *I remember girls in fifth grade being boy-crazy, chasing guys and going to their houses. I didn't understand why they were crazed. I felt different because I was painfully skinny, tiny, and underdeveloped. I never could eat enough and was trying to gain weight. I was almost a full year behind everyone else. They were in bras and using deodorant, and I was flat as a board and wore an undershirt. My dad even took me to the doctor and had my bones X-rayed because he was so worried. I didn't grow until the end of high school.*
>
> **–Lesley Seymour, former Editor-in-Chief, REDBOOK magazine**

When Your Self-Esteem Depends on Boyfriends

Some girls you know don't care about having a romantic relationship right now. Others think about it a lot. In part, your interest depends on your physical growth. Your body (through things like hormones and brain development) helps determine when you will become interested in romance. Everyone develops at a different rate.

In general, girls mature earlier than boys do. That means their bodies and emotions may tell them to become interested in romance before boys' bodies and emotions send out a similar signal to them. So if your self-esteem is dependent on how many boys like you, you could have a problem. Some of the nicest guys you know may not even have noticed that girls exist. Some won't be interested in having a girlfriend until high school or college. And some may never be interested in girls as girlfriends, just as some girls may never be interested in boys as boyfriends. Other boys may only like girls who they think aren't as smart as they are. Others may only like girls who are very thin, or have a certain color hair, or are a certain height. Boys who judge you by superficial traits like these can hurt you and your self-esteem if you let them. That's because they're only focusing on a small part of who you are.

There's no rush to start having boyfriends. Some girls, as a matter of fact, focus their attentions on other things until they are much older. Lesley Seymour, former editor-in-chief of *Redbook* magazine, for example, was almost seventeen before she thought about dating anyone.

If you do feel ready (or almost ready) for boyfriends, look for someone who shares your interests and who truly wants to get to know *you*. If it seems that in order to attract someone you have to . . .

• appear less smart or talented than you are

• lose weight and wear makeup and sexy clothes

• drink alcohol

• try cigarettes or marijuana

• let someone kiss or touch you when this doesn't feel right to you

. . . then it's not the right relationship for you.

Boyfriends can be exciting, which makes it hard to act sensibly. But play it smart and be an I CAN girl: Put your self-respect, confidence, and interests first. If you want others to value you, first and foremost you have to value yourself!

Can Your Self-Esteem Be Too High?

If you think you're wonderful at everything, you may have an inflated view of yourself. Kids who think they're the prettiest, smartest, or most athletic can be a pain in the brain to almost everyone around them—especially if they think it's cool to put others down. They risk turning other people away instead of making and keeping friends!

Even if you *are* really talented (or creative, or smart, or successful) realize that there will always be other people in the world who are even more talented (or creative, or whatever). You may not have met them yet, but you will. And when you do, your self-esteem will take a nosedive if it depends on believing that you—and only you—are the best. Sooner or later, you'll have to readjust your thinking, and you'll probably feel awkward, confused, or even sad until you get used to the idea of a less-than-perfect you.

But when you're both proud of and humble about your talents—when you perform well, work hard, and take pleasure in your abilities without bragging—then your self-esteem is based on a realistic view of yourself. So you're not likely to hurt other people's feelings when you demonstrate your abilities. You're not likely to feel as hurt when you see someone else succeed. You may even find that it feels good to compliment others for the things they achieve.

> *I believe we need to keep encouraging girls to take risks, make commitments, and achieve. We need to teach girls to have the courage to keep trying and to be vital members of our society, and that's an important part of the contribution I want to make.*
>
> **–Susan Lemagie, M.D., Obstetrician-Gynecologist and Women's Health Activist**

Accepting Yourself As You Are

Imagine what a boring world this would be if everyone were perfect! Without our "flaws," no one would have anything new to learn. No one would find ways to improve themselves and grow. But if you're not perfect, it's healthy to accept things about yourself that you don't like but can't—or have not yet been able to—change.

How can you start to feel good about those aspects of yourself? It may help to remember that no one is perfect. As a matter of fact, plenty of people probably share your imperfections. If you can, try to meet some of these people. For example, if you feel bad because you're not a big risk-taker, have a learning disability, live with a long-term disease, or don't like your curly hair, straight hair, height, weight, nose, or breasts, try to meet other people who are like you in that way. Some of them may turn out to be happy about things that bother you. Don't like your freckles? Some people feel their freckles make them stand out in a crowd. Wish you were more daring? Some people think it's good to play it safe.

Even a serious disability can be a blessing if you choose to see it that way. After her left hand got caught in a revolving saw when she was fourteen, New Jersey State Assemblywoman Mary Previte had to learn to braid her hair and ride a bicycle with one hand. But whenever she felt sorry for herself or said she couldn't do something, her dad would

say, "Well, I don't see why not!" Knowing that her dad believed in her helped Mary believe in herself. She says now that her disability made her more sensitive to others and taught her that she could overcome just about any obstacle.

Another thing you can do when you're critical of yourself is take a reality check: Are you comparing yourself with others? If you are, remind yourself that you're not the only one with flaws. *Everyone* has them. Instead of feeling bad about what you *don't* have or *can't* do, focus on your strengths. What can you do that other people value? What can you do that *you* value?

If you feel sad and these tips don't help you feel better, talk to a parent, teacher, school counselor, or other adult you trust about whatever is bothering you. They may have additional suggestions, and just talking about what's on your mind can be a big help.

A Better You = A Better World

Here's one other thing you can do to stay positive about yourself, and it may surprise you: Spend some time helping somebody else! Many successful *See Jane Win* women say that they feel most fulfilled and happiest with themselves when they're helping others or doing something to make the world a better place. Public radio host Kathleen Dunn, for example, is proud that, as a former VISTA volunteer, she spent two years helping low-income families. And Congresswoman Shelley

Berkley is such a strong believer in the importance of volunteering that she sponsored legislation aimed at encouraging people to do it even more.

Kids are capable of making a big difference in the world. For example, Marilyn Carlson Nelson learned how she could make a difference at her Sunday school when she was growing up. (Read the story on page 26 to find out how.) Young people raised millions of dollars when President George W. Bush asked every child to contribute a dollar to the children of Afghanistan. And a girl I know named Hannah has made it a birthday tradition to raise money for a different cause every year. Rather than get presents, she asks her friends to contribute to the charity of her choice instead.

I always wanted to help poor people. One day when I was ten, my family drove to Indianapolis. We were crossing the White River when I saw large, dark, looming structures that looked scary and threatening to me. I asked my parents what those buildings were, and they explained that they were the "projects" designed for poor people. I said, "I want to help those poor people get out." My parents told this story repeatedly, and my desire to empower people with limited resources has been a life goal.

–Norine Johnson, Ph.D., Clinical Psychologist and former President of the American Psychological Association

There are many good causes in the world for you to get involved in if you'd like! For a list of some ideas, see page 119.

Once you've selected a project, find some friends who are interested in working on it with you. Together, brainstorm some things that you could do:

KATIE & ILONNA'S CAMPAIGN TO IMPROVE SCHOOL READING

1. RUN A CAR WASH TO BUY BOOKS FOR CHILDREN.

2. ORGANIZE FRIENDS TO TUTOR YOUNGER CHILDREN IN READING.

3. TAKE TURNS READING TO KINDERGARTNERS.

4. MAKE POSTERS AND SIGN-UP SHEETS FOR PARENT VOLUNTEERS TO HELP KIDS READ.

5. WRITE A LETTER TO THE SCHOOL BOARD ASKING THEM TO PLEASE PUT MORE MONEY ASIDE FOR EXTRA READING TEACHERS AND MORE LIBRARY BOOKS.

6. ARRANGE WITH PRINCIPAL TO TALK TO LOCAL RESTAURANT ABOUT OFFERING SNACK COUPONS TO KIDS WHO READ 20 OR MORE BOOKS.

7. ASK ART TEACHER IF KIDS IN THE SCHOOL CAN MAKE POSTERS ABOUT THEIR FAVORITE BOOKS.

MIRIAM, LEILA, & DELLA'S PLAN TO HELP A DAYCARE CENTER

1. SPONSOR A TOY COLLECTION CAMPAIGN IN SCHOOL FOR THE DAYCARE CENTER.

2. GET FRIENDS TO HAVE A PICTURE EXCHANGE WITH CHILDREN AT THE CENTER.

3. ARRANGE TO READ TO CHILDREN AT THE DAYCARE CENTER.

4. SELL COOKIES, PIZZA, WRAPPING PAPER, OR ANOTHER ITEM TO BUY NEW TOYS FOR THE KIDS THERE.

Your ideas may not always be wildly successful but you can still make a difference. When you worry less about yourself and more about helping others, you'll be amazed how much you can achieve—and how good it can feel—to be an I CAN girl!

I believe one person can make a difference, and public service gives me the opportunity to give back something to this country that has given my family so much. That is the very essence and core of what I do and why I do it. I'm extraordinarily patriotic because I know what this country has done for my family, and I know we are just one of millions of families who would agree.

–Shelley Berkley, U.S. Congresswoman from Nevada

When I was twelve, I told my parents I wouldn't go to Sunday school anymore because I hated it. The boys shot spit wads and chased the girls around, and the Sunday school teacher couldn't control the class.

My father was furious. He declared, "You will go to Sunday school."

I retorted, "I won't. You don't want me to. It's a ridiculous waste of time."

He said, "Then fix it."

I cried and said, "What do you mean, 'Fix it?'"

My mother said, "Curt, leave her alone. You don't understand."

"No, I won't," he said. "If she doesn't like it, she has to fix it."

I kept saying, "I'm only twelve. It's a huge Sunday school. What can I do?"

He said, "That's the story of life. The forces are always bigger than you are, and one person can make a difference. If you don't, better that you go down trying than to not attempt it."

It never occurred to him that I couldn't change Sunday school. He sent me to my room to write a list of ideas. I had to call the superintendent and make an appointment to discuss my recommendations. We got some other young people involved and fixed Sunday school. The experience was very powerful.

–Marilyn Carlson Nelson, Chairman of the Board and Chief Executive Officer, Carlson Companies

Trying to make the world better for people and addressing the injustices of the world has been my lifelong passion.
–Kathleen Dunn, Public Radio Host

I CAN!

Tips for How You Can Develop Healthy Self-Esteem

- Turn down negative voices in your head. Believe in yourself!

- Use your strengths and show your talents—don't hide what you can do.

- Accept your weaknesses.

- Keep things in balance—be both proud and humble.

- Ask for help if you need it.

- Do your best at the things that are important to you.

- Remember that mistakes and setbacks don't mean you've failed. They're just a part of life.

- Be persistent.

- Give back by helping those who need it. Work alone and with others to fix problems and make improvements at school, in the community, and in the world.

- Set goals and work to make changes that develop your talents and abilities and help you to respect and like yourself.

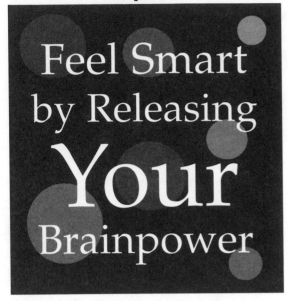

Chapter 3

Feel Smart by Releasing Your Brainpower

Do you feel smart? Are you always the first one to raise your hand when teachers ask a question? Do you have all the right answers when you turn on a TV game show? Even if you answered no to both questions, you may be smarter than you think. Intelligence shows itself in many ways, experts say. Some people are good at reading and writing, or math, or science, or logical thinking. (These are the kinds of smarts that get measured on tests at school.) Others get along well with all different types of people. This is a type of intelligence, too. Still others are smart in the ways they create or respond to music, art, or nature, or in the ways they think or see. Some are good with technology or machines. Some people are heart-smart—they have a special way of understanding feelings. And that's just a short list of the many types of intelligence in the world!

It's one thing to *be* smart. It's another to *use* your intelligence. One of the most important parts of being smart has to do with I CAN attitudes like enthusiasm, optimism, and a willingness to learn. The successful women in *See Jane Win* discovered that the smarter they felt, the more willing they were to use their brainpower to keep getting smarter.

Feeding Your Brain with Books

If you're a good reader, you probably feel pretty smart already. If you're not a good reader, crack open a book, anyway. Reading—even when it's hard for you—feeds your brain.

When heart surgeon Ana Casa* immigrated to the United States from the Dominican Republic as a child, she was confused about languages. Her native language was Spanish, and it took a while before she could truly call English her own. Sometimes she'd even get confused about which language she was using when!

Then, in third grade, Ana discovered her neighborhood public library. A whole new world of books opened up to her. She started reading four or five books a week. Suddenly she went from feeling different because she spoke a different language to feeling different because of how much she loved reading. The books not only helped her master English, they made her feel smarter than she had ever felt before.

> *I identified primarily with my father, who introduced us to reading. There were always books around our house, which transported us into another world, and we read anything we could get our hands on, from Nancy Drew mysteries to* One Flew Over the Cuckoo's Nest.
>
> **—Wilma P. Mankiller, former Principal Chief, Cherokee Nation**

> *School was easy for me. I was able to excel in all the subjects and loved to read and learn. In fifth grade, I wrote to a children's author, Madeleine L'Engle, because I wanted to be a writer and illustrator like her.*
>
> **—Connie Matsui, Senior Vice President, Planning and Resource Development, IDEC Pharmaceuticals; and National President, Girl Scouts of the USA**

Many of the women in *See Jane Win* felt smart in elementary school because they were active readers. Neurosurgeon Alexa Canady loved to read—ten or twelve little blue biographies a week. She skipped a grade. Congresswoman Nydia Velázquez also skipped a grade. She begged for and read encyclopedias and thought she could become an intellectual.

Many of the women especially loved reading stories about women who followed their dreams, like war nurse Florence Nightingale; abolitionist Sojourner Truth; aviator Amelia Earhart; and Helen Keller, who learned to read even though she was blind and deaf. Space shuttle commander Eileen Collins was thrilled when she found books about Jacqueline Cochran, a female pilot who grew up in poverty. Psychologist Dr. Anne Caroles* was motivated to do her best in school—and particularly in science—after reading a biography of Nobel Prize–winning scientist Marie Curie. Senator Kay Bailey Hutchison read all the biographies in her school's library. And reading was so important to talk show host Oprah Winfrey that she made it a point to share favorite books with others on her television show.

Many books about extraordinary women are on store and library shelves for you to choose from. Ask a librarian for suggestions if you have trouble finding them on your own.

How to Become an I CAN Bookworm

Feel you're not reading enough? Here are some ideas that may inspire you to "book it" to a local library or bookstore more than you do now.

Indulge your interests: Find out more about topics you already find fascinating. If you love horses, look for books about different breeds, or training, or racing, as well as fiction about horses to spur your imagination. If chess is your thing, read books about famous chess matches, or titles about how to improve your game. Like making crafts? Look for books and magazines with patterns, ideas, instructions, and suggestions.

Expand your reading horizons: Try a mix of biographies, adventure stories, mysteries, historical fiction, and science-related titles. When you find a type of book you like, read others like it until you feel that you need a change.

Hold a family read-aloud: Ask a parent, grandparent, aunt, or uncle to share books with you that they loved as children. Then share your own favorites with sisters, brothers, cousins, and other members of your family.

Make reading a habit: Find a special time and place to treat yourself to a good book—in bed before you go to sleep, out in the park on a quiet weekend morning, or after your homework is done. Or find some other private reading spot to call your own.

> *I lived in a small town, but because of my reading and exposure, I knew there was a bigger world out there. There were no libraries or bookstores, but my parents and I traveled to larger cities, where I could buy books. While my mother shopped, she would find me sitting on the floor in the book department, reading books. If we visited someone, the first thing I'd look for in their house was a book. I've always been an avid reader and writer, and I would look through magazines for the kind of house that I was going to have one day. I'd tear photos of furniture from catalogs, and I kept a travel journal.*
>
> **–Marva Collins, Founder, Marva Collins Preparatory School, Chicago**

Find a book buddy: Trade favorite books with a friend. Then pick one book you both like and turn it into a play to perform for your class, neighborhood, club, or youth group. That may get others excited about reading it, too.

Author, author: When you fall in love with a book, check out others by the same writer. If you like, write the author a letter or an email explaining what you like about the books. (You can write to an author in care of his or her publisher. Look for the publisher's address or Web site on the copyright page at the beginning of the book.) Who knows? You may even hear back!

> *Growing up, I read everything I could get my hands on. I loved going to the library and was always asking the librarian for recommendations. If there was anything I was interested in knowing more about, she could find a book to show me the way. It's no wonder that my love of books—knowing how they can inform and inspire young readers—led me to start my own successful publishing company!*
>
> **–Judy Galbraith, Founder and President, Free Spirit Publishing Inc.**

Don't stop with books: When you look for something new to read, don't forget about the wide variety of magazines, newspapers, and webzines that you can choose from. Once you get hooked on reading, you'll find that there's never a shortage of new things to read!

Breaking Math and Science Stereotypes

If you're one of those kids who stares at your math and science textbook wondering, "When will I ever need to know this stuff?" just look around! You can't budget your allowance, calculate the bucks you get from baby-sitting, split the cost of a pizza, or start your own business without mathematics. And without scientists and inventors, there would be no TVs, computers, light switches, or medicines to help you when you're sick. Most interesting careers—and most of our daily lives—require a knowledge of these subjects.

Just look at what some of the *See Jane Win* women have accomplished using their math and science know-how: NASA astronaut Cady Coleman used hers to log over 500 hours in space, e-publisher Annik LaFarge couldn't bring books to the Internet without it, and knowledge of these subjects has allowed neurosurgeon Alexa Canady to save many children's lives. If you have ever thought of becoming a veterinarian, architect, schoolteacher, interior designer, astronaut, graphic artist, or doctor, then you'll *really* need them.

> *My fifth- and sixth-grade teachers turned me on to science and didn't segregate girls from boys in anything. My fifth-grade teacher had us wire a dollhouse so we could actually see how electricity lit up the house and turned on buzzers. He also had us wire the internal organs of the body on a big board he had colored. Science literally lit up for us!*
>
> **–Sandra Labas Fenwick, Chief Operations Officer, Children's Hospital, Boston**

Some people believe that girls can never be as good as boys at math or science. Others say that anyone who likes these subjects is a nerd. But don't believe them! Right in your own school, lots of girls are interested in these subjects—and their grades are every bit as good as boys' are. You may even be one of them. And if you need proof that these subjects are cool, think about this: *Friends* actress Lisa Kudrow, Olympic softball player Dot Richardson, and *The Wonder Years* actress Danica McKellar all graduated from college with degrees in these subject areas!

Don't be fooled into thinking that for some kids these subjects are easy. Granted, for a lucky few they're *fairly* easy—just as another subject may be fairly easy for you. But most kids who seem to breeze through science and math study really hard. By middle school, high school, or college, even the strongest math and science students find that the subjects aren't as easy as they once were. Catherine Burns* was always confident about her abilities in mathematics—until she became a graduate student at the Massachusetts Institute of Technology. For the first time ever, she worried that she was the only one having a hard time in her math classes. But she persevered. And now she teaches engineering, which includes lots of math, at this very prestigious college!

So take up the challenge! What better way can you find to prove how capable you are than by mastering a tough subject? Even if you don't ace every test, you can do your best. And remember to give yourself credit for how much you've learned.

I CAN Experiments in Math and Science

Does the sight of a math textbook send a shiver of panic up your spine? Does the thought of dissecting a frog turn you greener than the frog itself? Take a deep breath, relax, and use these ideas to put yourself at ease.

Start your own business: Nothing makes numbers as interesting as earning money. One day, when she was in third grade, Tamara Minick-Scokalo, now marketing director at Procter & Gamble, shared a bag of jelly beans with her friends at recess. That gave her an idea. Borrowing $25 from her dad, she bought more jelly beans and other snacks, and she sorted them into small plastic bags and began selling them at recess. Suddenly she was in business! Before long, Tamara had paid her dad back, along with interest on the money he'd lent her, and was making a profit. You too can earn extra money by thinking of a product to sell—your own sports drink, garden vegetables, or tie-dyed T-shirts, but if you want to sell it in school, first you need to get permission from your principal. Or maybe you can make some cash by doing special chores around your home—by baby-sitting, dog-walking, leaf-raking, or garage-cleaning for a neighbor. Estimate what, if anything, it will cost to start your business, and arrange for a loan if you need one. Then calculate your profits as they start to add up!

Cook up a storm: Recipe books are full of fractions and measurements. And mixing ingredients in the kitchen is not so different  from mixing chemicals in a lab. So find a dinner or dessert recipe that sounds good and give it a shot! First check to make sure you have all the ingredients. Then multiply or divide the recipe so you make just the right amount for your family or friends. Check with your mom or dad before you use the oven or stove. And clean up when you're done. Then chow down. What a great math/science treat!

Play ball!: Volunteer to be official score-keeper at the bowling alley, the baseball field, or the basketball court. Before long, you'll be a real whiz at adding numbers in your head!

Raise money for a good cause: As a girl, Susan Widham (former president of the Beech-Nut Nutrition Corporation) sold more candy than anyone else in her Campfire Girls troop, even though she considered herself very shy. If you take on a similar fund-raising project, keep a record of how much you collect. And don't be surprised if you find yourself working even harder than you would if the money was just for you.

Play card and board games: Many card games and board games require mathe-matical thinking and problem solving. So invite a friend over and practice your math skills in an incredibly painless way. Such a sacrifice for math!

Play teacher for a day: The best way to understand something is to explain it. Helping a little kid memorize the multi-plication tables, demonstrating how the earth rotates around the sun, or what the difference is between two- and three-dimensional shapes can help you improve your own math and science skills.

Be a shopping helper: Check local news-papers for coupons of products that your family often buys, and then offer to do the shopping. Or ask neighbors—particularly older people who may have trouble get-ting to the store—if they'd like you to shop for them. Challenge yourself to find the best buys, and then figure out how much money you've saved. Show everyone what a savvy consumer you can be!

Plant a garden: Plant seeds for different kinds of plants. You can plant them in a garden plot or in pots placed on a patio or windowsill. Care for your plants as they grow. Do they like a lot of sun or a little? Do research about your plants. What kinds of insects do they attract? Keep a garden journal with findings and sketches of your garden's progress.

Teach your old pet new tricks: See how long it takes for your hamster or pet mouse to find its way through a maze. Figure out how to train your cat to come when you call. Teach your dog to roll over. Keep a log of the results—just as any good scientist would— because you're studying animal behavior.

Get Off to the "Write" Start

When I was in eighth grade, I had to give a report on the slave trade from Africa. I had trouble figuring out how to start it. Finally I decided to write the report as if I had been forced onto a slave ship myself. When I stood up to read, I was nervous. The class hadn't paid much attention to the other kids. But when I began telling the story of being captured and taken from my imaginary family, the class grew totally silent. Everybody was moved by my report, and the teacher gave me an A+.

It's amazing how the confidence gained from an experience like this can stay with a person. Even today, when I'm better known as a child psychologist than as a writer, this book is proof of how much I still love to write! And I'm not the only one. Best-selling author Jacquelyn Mitchard wrote whenever possible when she was growing up. After everyone in her family had gone to bed, she lay on the floor and wrote, using light that shone under her door. She also wrote for school newspapers whenever she could, and she considered the authors of books to be among her best friends.

But even if writing is not your favorite hobby, it's guaranteed to come in handy, no matter what you do. Whether you want to be a scientist, a politician, a nurse, an architect, a business executive, a computer programmer, a movie director, a fashion designer, a salesperson, or a mother—you name it—you will probably have to do some writing. It may take the form of notes, emails, letters, business reports, research papers, or shopping lists and lists of things to do for your home, but you will need to write.

Write On!

Writing doesn't have to mean boring essays, uninspired book reports, or tedious school research papers! Here are some creative ways to express yourself with a pen and paper or computer:

Keep a journal or diary: A journal or diary is a friend you can always count on, no matter what! Use yours to describe your activities and, more importantly, your feelings. Every day will be different. Sometimes you'll write just a sentence, other times a whole page. Read *The Diary of Anne Frank, The Diary of Latoya Hunter,* and other published diaries of real people to get an idea of how other girls used theirs.

Create a family newsletter: Do you or others in your family have some news that's worth sharing: A family outing or trip to tell about? A new baby or some holiday cheer you'd like to send? A family newsletter is a great way to do it. You might interview family members, share happy memories, or even include a made-up story. Consider putting out an issue monthly, or once every season.

Bring some imagination to school reports: Just as I imagined being forced into slavery when I put together my eighth-grade report, so can you pretend to live in another country or time period when you write a paper for school. You might imagine that you're a time traveler from the future, or try to figure out how you'd feel and what you would do if you were in some famous person's shoes.

Write yourself into a favorite book or movie: What would it be like to hang out with Harriet the Spy, Stuart Little, Mulan, or another favorite book or movie character? Write a story about what might happen, and see where the story leads!

Stay in touch with friends: Even if you just saw your best friend an hour  ago, you can still sit down and write her a letter or an email about what's happening. You might even make up things and tell about those, too. Just be sure your friend knows which parts are imaginary and which are for real!

Speak your mind on paper: Write a letter to the editor of your school or local newspaper on a topic that matters to you. Or write to the President, another public official, a movie or television star, or someone you know who could use some cheering up. Tell that person whatever is on your mind. Then watch your mailbox. You may just get a reply!

Try your hand at poetry: Poetry and rhymes can help you to express yourself, whether your mood is sad or silly. Playing with words will stretch your thinking and help you to explain what you're feeling.

Enter a contest or try publishing: Ask an adult to help you find a writing contest for kids, or magazines that publish poems and stories by people your age. You may not always win or get published, but don't give up! J.K. Rowling (author of the Harry Potter books) and other well-known authors received lots of rejections before they finally saw their words in print. But author Susan Eloise (S.E.) Hinton had her first book, *The Outsiders*, published when she was just seventeen years old, and Helen Gurley Brown, former editor-in-chief of *Cosmopolitan* magazine, published her first story when she was eight.

Art Smarts: You and Your Creativity

So far we've looked at smarts related to reading, writing, math, and science—all highly creative fields in their own ways. But many *See Jane Win* women have fond memories of being recognized for their smarts as painters, actors, dancers, or musicians. By the time they were in middle school, some had even earned labels like "the artist," "the dancer," or "the musician," helping them see how their talents could make them stand out in a crowd. Mary GrandPré, now known for her Harry Potter illustrations, sold her first works of art in middle school when she displayed her drawings at a local church bazaar. Graphic artist Rodene Brchan made artistic gifts for her friends at about the same age. Janet Schiller, a producer for NBC's *Today* show, was a serious dancer as a child and young adult. She changed careers later, but she says her ballet training set her apart in ways that made her feel smart and helped build her confidence.

> I was less social than most and sometimes felt isolated. Art was my outlet. My work was exhibited in school, and I won art contests. Surprisingly, my English teacher influenced me as much as my art teachers. I would illustrate authors, poets, literature, and receive much encouragement for my artwork as I applied it to English. Art was all-important and helped me cope with my isolation.
>
> **–Donna Jacobsen,**
> **Artist and Illustrator**

Not all the creative abilities that the women I interviewed remember being recognized for were about art, dance, or music. Sometimes it was a creative way of thinking or looking at the world that helped them to gain confidence. Patricia Seybold, the chief executive officer of an Internet consulting company and a best-selling author, organized theater projects with neighborhood friends as a child. They produced plays and circuses and collected money (usually about a nickel from each audience member) to benefit worthy causes. She gained confidence and practiced her leadership skills, while having fun at the same time.

Magazine editor Lesley Seymour described herself as a worker bee. She loved to be involved in many things at the same time. She took pride in being able to do so much when other people would be overwhelmed, and it made her feel that she could do anything she set her mind to.

As a young writer working for the magazine *Vogue*, Lesley was asked to write a regular column about automobiles. She loved the idea, but she didn't know how to drive! Instead of letting that stop her, she signed up for driving lessons the next day.

Not long after she got her license, Lesley was offered the chance to drive a new, ultra-expensive sports car. Before she knew it, she was out on the highway in a bright red two-seater going only thirty-five miles per hour! When someone with her asked why she was driving so slowly in a vehicle known for its speed, she had to admit that she'd just learned to drive and was afraid to go any faster.

Now that shows what a creative, determined, truly gutsy, and very honest I CAN girl can achieve!

Being Smart About Learning Differences

Lots of students have some kind of learning difference, which is sometimes called a learning disability, or LD. Having a learning difference or disability doesn't mean you aren't smart. It simply means that you learn in different ways and may need some special help to learn as much or as fast as others. It means that some school subjects or tasks may not come that easily to you.

> As I look back at it now, I believe feeling unsuccessful may be a key to becoming successful. Learning to overcome self-doubt and self-consciousness is a very powerful and transforming experience. You become stronger and more resilient than if everything comes easily and without challenge.
>
> **–Connie Matsui, Senior Vice President, Planning and Resource Development, IDEC Pharmaceuticals; and National President, Girl Scouts of the USA**

Take Martha Lindner, for example. Despite a reading disability called dyslexia, Martha is a happy and successful lawyer today. In school, she had to work three times as long as other students to finish the same amount of reading. But as an I CAN girl, she turned her disadvantage to an advantage. To overcome her reading challenges, Martha read things over and over again until she understood them. She read slowly—but carefully. She also asked her teacher for help with her reading skills. Both her thoroughness and her ability to reach out to others come in handy in her profession.

> It's important for all young people, particularly women, to realize that sometimes what you think is the worst thing that ever happened to you turns out to be the best thing.
>
> **–Martha Lindner, Attorney**

Other women I interviewed said math and science were their toughest subjects. But they all found that persistence and hard work paid off. Some asked a parent, older neighbor, brother, or sister to tutor them. Others, who were talented in art, music, or drama, used these strengths to give their grades a boost. For example, if music is your passion, see if you can improve your history grade by writing a report about the instruments, types of music, or songs that were popular during the time period your class is studying. If you're a good artist, you might earn extra science credit by creating a detailed diagram showing the earth's water cycle or the various types of clouds. Graphic artist Rodene Brchan used her art abilities in similar ways when she was in elementary school. She made such an impression that her sixth-grade art and science teacher invited her back to teach his class for a day after she'd gone on to high school.

It's sometimes tempting to ignore hard assignments or make excuses, but that won't help you feel smarter. You'll only fall further behind and then feel worse—even if you pretend you don't care. It's better to find help and get back on track. You'll learn more and begin to feel much better about your I CAN girl self!

I had chronic bronchitis as a kid, so I missed a lot of school and my grades began to slip. When my oldest brother found out I was getting a D in algebra, he had a fit. He made me get out of bed every morning at 6 A.M. and sit at the dining room table. He said, "You're not doing your homework. Nobody gets a D in algebra unless they don't do their homework." He helped me get through it. That completely turned my grade around.

–Lisa Smith*, Research Chemist

An Apple for the Teacher

If you believe in your teachers, there's a good chance that they'll believe in you. All you have to do is respect them and show them how much you want to learn. As the tributes on these pages show, most teachers want very much to inspire their students. And you have the power to help them do that. If you need help, ask for it. If you have special interests or needs, let them know that, too. A teacher's encouragement can have a huge influence in helping you to be your best.

My goal was to become a high school math teacher because my math teachers were really inspiring female role models. I fell in love with economics when I took an elective class, and my teacher was absolutely outstanding.

–Katherine Hudson, President and Chief Executive Officer, the Brady Corporation

My seventh-grade English teacher was Mrs. Hardy. Her expectations were very high. Everyone was terrified of her, but I always wanted to please her. She introduced me to poetry, to speaking grammatically, and to striving to do more. She was hard but fair, and it meant so much to me to do well in her class. She was responsible for my yearning to want to be the best.

–Deborah Roberts, Correspondent, ABC's 20/20 Newsmagazine

My fourth-grade teacher, Edith Turner, probably had more impact on my life than anyone. She was generations ahead of her time for travel, adventure, the love of the earth, and ecology, and she took us on imaginary adventures all over the world. We did a project on Antarctica way back then, and I knew I had to visit there someday.

–Frances Bayless, Wildlife Photographer

I loved my teachers. One day when I was in kindergarten I realized I'd forgotten to wear my underwear, and I wouldn't take my snow pants off. My teacher asked, "What's wrong?" and I explained, with great embarrassment. She was so kind and made everything all right so no one would make fun of me or ask questions. I thought teachers were wonderful people. I wanted to be like them.

–Lisa Hayes-Taylor, Elementary School Teacher

I CAN!

Tips for How You Can
Make the Best Use of Your Brainpower

- Be optimistic and enthusiastic about schoolwork. Show that you're ready and willing to learn.

- Read as much as you can.

- Practice good study habits—and don't give up, even when a topic is hard for you.

- Form a study group with your friends. You can help them with the subjects you're good at, and they can help you with the ones they're good at.

- Find ways to use math, science, and other school subjects in your everyday life.

- See how creative you can be when it comes to writing stories and reports for school.

- Keep a journal, and look for other ways to sharpen your writing skills.

- Learn as much as you can from your teachers.

- Use your mental strengths to make up for any weaknesses you have.

- If you need help, ask!

Chapter 4

Improving Your Social Smarts

Using your creativity and doing well on tests are only two ways to show your intelligence. Traits like kindness, sensitivity, good social skills, independence, strong leadership abilities, and showing what a trusted friend you can be may not show up on your report card. But they have led to success in life for many I CAN girls.

Friends to the End

Are you the type who has one or two best friends who you share your secret thoughts and confidences with? If so, you probably enjoy the sense of closeness that it brings. It's great to have people in your life that you can rely on . . . and to know they feel that way about you, too.

On the other hand, if you like to be around large groups of people and enjoy having many friends, you'd probably describe yourself as very social—maybe even popular. But when you're with more than four or five kids at a time, you may be less willing to share anything personal. That's understandable. After all, secrets don't stay secret very long in big groups.

Some people are popular or socialize with lots of kids, because of their kindness, leadership ability, great personality, and other wonderful traits. But some people's popularity comes from hanging around kids who bully, embarrass, gossip about, or exclude others, or who do unhealthy things like drink or smoke. That's not so wonderful. This kind of popularity can get you into trouble—and leave you feeling bad about yourself.

Television news anchor Donna Draves* learned this when she was in middle school. She and her two best friends would go to a local theme park to smoke, hang out, and look for boys. At that time in her life, popularity was so important to her that she was willing to get into trouble with her parents and at school just to be with these kids.

Then an inspiring teacher convinced Donna to enter a speech contest. She won, which motivated her to continue in speech. Gradually other kids who were good students and had more positive values started to accept her. She began to realize that she could be true to herself and her own interests and still have a good time and plenty of friends.

It's great to have both close friends and more casual friends—people who make you feel comfortable, share your interests, and are fun to be with. But just because you wouldn't call some people friends doesn't mean they have to be your enemies. You can still get along with them, too. Knowing who your real friends are—and who to count on for what—is just a part of what social smarts, or social intelligence, is all about.

And the Survey Says:
Many of the successful women in *See Jane Win* described themselves as independent when they were growing up.

Taking Time for Yourself

It's good to have family and friends to hang out with, but an I CAN girl is also proud of her independence. Being independent means taking time to be on your own, and making sure that you're not always ruled by what others say and do. When you're independent, you're comfortable with yourself—even if that means doing things you want to do when no one else is around to go with you.

Independence also means taking responsibility for your actions. That includes knowing who and when to ask for help, when you can take care of things on your own, and how to make good choices. If you're independent, you know that within the guidelines set by the adults in your life, you have the freedom to think for yourself.

Being independent also means being strong enough to tell friends when you want some privacy. This can be hard—especially when a close friend really wants you around. When this happens, be honest. Say something like, "Tracy, you know I love to hang out with you, and we can get together tomorrow, but today I need to do some things by myself." There are probably times when she needs to be by herself, too.

Tracy may be disappointed, but hopefully she'll understand. There's more chance of hurting her feelings—and your friendship—if you lie or make up excuses (or ask others to do that for you) and she finds out. If you don't reject her invitations very often and she still doesn't understand . . . well, then there's not much more you can do.

Independence can sometimes be scary. It takes confidence and courage to do the right thing and stand up to others when you disagree with them. When you're independent, you follow your own personal path—even when others tease or exclude you for not doing the same things as them.

Some On-Your-Own Activities to Try

Some kids just naturally find things they enjoy doing by themselves. Others get antsy—or even sad and lonely—if they're alone for long. If this describes you, find some activities you enjoy. (See the following list for ideas.) Build up the amount of time you spend doing them on your own. You may find that you enjoy this time by yourself more and more!

- Read a book

- Write in your journal

- Explore your neighborhood—and bring a camera or sketchbook along to record what you see

- Create a scrapbook on your favorite topic

- Practice playing a musical instrument

- Listen to music—especially types you don't usually listen to

- Write an original play or story

- Make a gift for someone

- Learn something new from an encyclopedia or on the Internet

- Play with your pet

- Invent something that will help a friend or family member

- Paint a picture

- Write a poem or song

- Reorganize your bedroom

- Create a new dance

- Take a bike ride

- Find a recipe you'd like to try and get permission to make it

- Work on a jigsaw puzzle

- Learn to knit, weave, embroider, or crochet

- Do a crossword puzzle

- Fly a kite

> *In middle school, I remember alternating between wanting to have a boyfriend and go to parties, and wanting to play baseball and climb trees. My friend had a baseball that had been signed by famous White Sox players, and we'd toss it to each other between classes. I never felt I had to be with the in crowd. I was trying out different roles, so it might have been a dress one day and blue jeans, a White Sox T-shirt, and a baseball cap the next.*
>
> **–Kathleen Dunn, Public Radio Host**

And the Survey Says:
Only about one in four of the women I interviewed in *See Jane Win* thought of themselves as very social or popular as kids. The rest fell into the average or less social group.

Can't We All Just Get Along?

Some girls enjoy being in large groups of people. Others prefer small groups or spending time alone. Most fall somewhere in between. Whatever you're like, if you're socially smart, you do your best to get along with all different types of people—and you avoid making assumptions about them because of how they look, act, or dress, or the types of things they like to do.

In many schools and neighborhoods, kids use labels like "jock," "preppy," and "brain." Then they form cliques—small groups of friends who only hang out with other kids they think of being like them.

But when you get to know someone well, you're likely to find that these labels don't mean much. No one's personality is so simple that it can be boiled down to one or two words. Who you are is influenced by many things: your neighborhood, your interests, your religion or lack of religion, your color, your sex, where you were born, your grandmother's cooking—the list is endless. One girl I know, Tanya, put it very well when she described herself as granola. "That means, like the cereal, I'm a mixture of many natural ingredients!"

Sure, you may become close to someone because you both like animals, or the same kinds of music, or have similar family backgrounds. You may also become friends with someone else because you like his smile, or how he acts or dresses, or how different he seems from you.

Maybe you're independent enough to ignore labels and be yourself—no matter what. But everyone is tempted at some point to go along with the crowd. That's what peer pressure is all about.

When people change themselves to fit in with a group, they're reacting to something called peer pressure. Maybe they start cursing, stealing, cheating, saying mean things, or calling people names. Maybe they laugh or say nothing at all when others are doing these things. Kids do it. And so do adults sometimes. If your friends gossip, drink, or smoke, you may feel that you have to join in. On the other hand, if you have friends who frown on these habits, you're less likely to do them yourself. So, there are actually times when peer pressure can be a good thing!

Being liked and accepted is important, but it isn't everything. I CAN girls know this. If you're selective and persistent, you can find loyal friends who like you *and* have positive values—friends who you can influence in a positive way and who will have a healthy influence on you.

> *Sometimes I'm quiet, but I've never been shy. I like having a lot of friends and like being with people as opposed to being alone. I learned a long time ago that if I walk up to a group of people and wait there for a second or two, then say, "Hi, I'm Cathie Black," generally, people will offer their name, and they will be pleasant and friendly.*
>
> **–Cathleen Black, President, Hearst Magazines**

Why Kids Can Be Mean

It's sad, but some people feel important when they pick on others. Although kids shouldn't treat other kids this way, it helps to understand why it happens and to know what you can do about it. If a mean person becomes a leader, that person may use the nasty things she or he says to control others. Kids who aren't in that group may feel pressure to be cruel so that they'll feel included, too. Or, they may be afraid that, if they don't join in, the leader will soon start picking on them.

If you ever find yourself accepted by kids who treat others badly, you may be tempted to act this way, too—even to kids who once were your friends. But do you really want to hang out with mean and disrespectful people—even if, at your school, they are considered the in crowd? After all, true friends would never push you to be mean to anyone else just so you could stay friends with them. So "do unto others as you would have them do unto you." Never treat anyone like an outcast!

What if you suddenly find yourself left out by someone who once was a good bud? Try talking to the person about how you feel. Say, "I want to be friends with you and I don't think I did anything to hurt you. I can't understand why you're suddenly being so mean to me. If you feel I'm doing something wrong, let's talk about it. Maybe together we can work it out." If your friend is truly a friend and is independent enough, the two of you should at least be able to have an honest conversation. If not, you'll still know that you did the right thing by trying to talk.

Remember how important it is to be independent. If the kids in a particular group won't accept you, try to ignore their meanness. Once they realize that they're not getting you down, they're likely to lose interest in being mean to you anyway. That's what happened to flutist Martha Aarons when she was in middle school. She was teased for being an excellent student and liking classical music. For a while she tried to learn more about popular music, but she still wasn't accepted. It wasn't until she attended a music camp the summer she was in eighth grade that she found a place where people had similar interests and she could be accepted for who she was. The name-calling stopped after that, or at least it didn't bother her as much anymore.

Rather than worry about the people who don't accept you, look for new friends who will. Get busy with things that interest you, like music, sports, or volunteer work. If you feel sad because

you don't have friends, talk to a school counselor about it. Maybe she can organize a friendship session to help the kids talk out their differences. You can also turn to an adult you feel close to— someone whose understanding can help get you through these difficult times.

If you find yourself threatened by more than name-calling, though, you can't just ignore it. If you're worried that a kid may hurt you physically, talk to an adult you trust right away.

When I was growing up, a neighborhood boy started picking on me, and it was clear that he wanted to fight. I sized him up and thought I could handle him. So I said, "I don't want to fight, but if you do, you might be in trouble."

Wham! That kid packed a wallop, and I ran home crying. So learn from my bruises: If you find yourself in a situation like mine, tell an adult in your home or at school.

Sure, other kids may say you're a tattletale if they find out, but that doesn't make you one. Tattling is when you tell on others to make it seem like you're the good kid and they're the bad ones. What you're doing is reporting, which has a higher purpose: preventing violence and keeping people safe.

> *My earliest memories of deciding who I was and what I wanted to do with my life go back to the fourth grade. I lived in Georgia and distinctly remember segregation, colored waiting rooms, and a colored school. When I moved to an integrated school, it was a time of nervousness, but also a time of wonder and exploration. I made friends with white children for the first time and realized that the big scary world wasn't as scary as I'd thought. I tried out for cheerleading in seventh grade and was upset because I didn't make it, so I tried again the next year and did. My activities emboldened me to feel like I could do well in the world.*
>
> **–Deborah Roberts, Correspondent, ABC's 20/20 Newsmagazine**

DEAR DR. SYLVIA:

An I CAN Q&A on Social Smarts

No matter how social you are, things are easier if you get along well with others. But if you don't feel comfortable with many other kids right now, that's okay! There's always time and room for growth and improvement. The answers to the I CAN girls' questions on these pages may also help you to improve your social skills.

Q. DEAR DR. SYLVIA: Kids are nice to me, but I just don't feel like part of the group. I feel really different. Sometimes I like being different because it makes me feel special and other times I hate it because it makes me feel so lonely. What should I do?

—ALONE IN A GROUP

A. Dear Alone in a Group: It's great to have special talents, unusual ideas, or unique interests that can help you define yourself as someone special and distinct from others. Original qualities like these help you know who you are—but they can sometimes cause you to feel lonely or different, too. Perhaps wearing clothes or hairstyles like your friends' could help you feel like you fit in better. There's nothing wrong with that as long as you're not copying kids who might take you in a direction you or your family wouldn't like. Talk to an adult you trust about any concerns you have. They can help you decide when it's good to conform to the crowd and when it's best to strike out on your own.

You might also see if you can find kids in a youth or community group, or at your place of worship, whose personalities and interests are more like yours. You may find you fit in better and feel more comfortable there. Being independent can take some getting used to. But successful I CAN girls believe in themselves and follow their own paths—even if it feels lonely sometimes.

Q. DEAR DR. SYLVIA: There are an odd number of girls in our class, so when the teacher asks us to take partners there's always one girl left over to be a partner with a boy. That always seems to be me. Do you have any ideas to help me change this?

—ODD ONE OUT

A. Dear Odd One Out: Maybe you could talk to your teacher privately and ask if she would allow one or two threesomes in the classroom.

Then you could choose which friends you work with and the extra boy could do the same thing. Or perhaps your teacher could make it a point to rotate which girl partners with a boy, or allow you to select your partner first sometimes. It doesn't hurt to ask! If the teacher is not willing to change her current system, keep an open mind and try to get to know your partner—whoever it is. Who knows? The two of you could even wind up becoming friends!

Q. DEAR DR. SYLVIA: I get invited to parties and have friends, but I feel uncomfortable and shy when I'm at a party with new people. I just can't seem to find things to talk about except when I'm with close friends who know me.

—WHAT SHOULD I SAY?

A. Dear what should I say?: Instead of worrying about being shy, think up some good questions and topics to talk about (like hobbies, movies, favorite music groups, or books you've read) before you head off to the party. If you can get other kids talking, the conversation may just start to flow. You might find it easier to introduce yourself to a small group of kids rather than to one person. There's less pressure that way. You can listen in on their conversation until you feel ready to add something. And if you know any good jokes, go ahead and tell them. When people laugh together, everyone begins to feel more relaxed.

Q. DEAR DR. SYLVIA: Boys in seventh and eighth grade seem to be friendly to me even though I'm only in sixth grade. In some ways I like it because I feel popular and other girls think I'm lucky. But I don't feel ready for a boyfriend yet. I know my body is developing earlier than many of my girlfriends'. I've heard boys make comments about that. Sometimes I'm so embarrassed I'd just like to hide and become smaller. I don't want to be liked just for my looks. My parents have made it clear that my intelligence and personality are more important, but I don't want to cover up my looks either. What do you think?

—EARLY BLOOMER

A. Dear Early Bloomer: There's nothing wrong with being both attractive and smart. There's also nothing wrong with making it clear to these older boys that you're not interested in having a boyfriend. Joining a girls' group, like Girl Scouts or Girls Inc., or a girls' sport, could take some pressure off you. So might hanging out with girls and boys who share your interests. Pretty soon the other girls will catch up with you in their development and you won't feel so different about your body anymore.

Developing Empathy and Sensitivity

Sympathy means being sensitive to other people's feelings. Empathy is being so sensitive that you almost get into that person's skin and feel what she feels. Understanding how others feel can help you solve problems—especially problems with other kids.

Understanding someone else's point of view doesn't necessarily mean that you change your opinions. Even best friends don't always see eye to eye. But it will help you understand where the other person is coming from. Sometimes, if there is a disagreement, being sympathetic can help you reach a compromise.

It takes a lot of listening to really grasp how another person is feeling— even if the other person is your best friend. But if you're an empathetic person, friends are likely to confide in you more often. Sometimes they'll confide a secret that's fun to share, but other secrets may be about things that worry or even frighten them. When that happens, all you have to do is listen and empathize— unless the secret is something that could put someone in danger, or one that terrifies you, too. For example, if your friend is shoplifting, is making herself vomit after meals, or is so sad that she's planning to hurt herself, then it's time to let an adult know right away.

You can tell your friend, "This problem is too serious for you or me to handle. I don't want to be unfair to you, but I have to tell an adult about this. I care too much about you to keep it to myself." Your friend may cry or get angry, but a true friend reports serious problems.

How Kind Is Too Kind?

Kindness can be a wonderful quality. It suggests that you're sensitive, understanding, empathetic, and good to others. People who are kind as children often grow into adults who continue to do good things.

But it's also possible to be too kind. For example, say a friend of yours is struggling in school and asks you to give her answers to a homework assignment. The kind part of you may be tempted— especially if you see that she doesn't learn

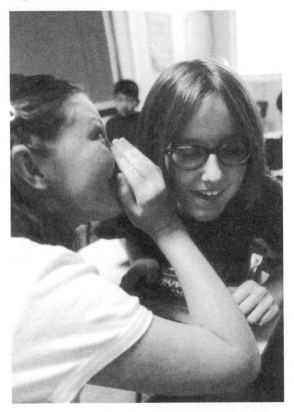

things as easily as you do. But if you give her your answers, she won't learn, and her schoolwork will suffer. This would hurt her confidence and self-esteem. Besides, the teacher could accuse you of cheating—which of course you would be. The truly kind thing to do is to tell your friend, "No, I can't give you the answers. But if you like, I'd be happy to help you figure it out."

Be prepared—your friend may get so annoyed, she may even want to stop being friends with you. But do you really want to hang onto a friend who not only wants you to cheat but who cuts you out of her life if you won't? Sometimes you have to say no to be true to yourself. Stay strong. Be clear about your values and make sure you take care of yourself.

Or take another example: suppose a friend asks you to stay at her house on Friday night, but your family usually plays board games on Friday night. Your dad travels a lot, so you want to be home because you haven't seen him all week. But you're afraid to hurt your friend's feelings because you're her best friend. What can you say? "Matriece, my dad just got back from traveling and I just want to be with the family. I don't want to hurt your feelings, but maybe we could get together tomorrow during the day and I could stay overnight another time."

It's better to be honest with your friend and not say things like "my mom won't let me come." If you make up stories, your friend won't trust you in the future. Honesty between friends is important.

Your friend may be disappointed, and that may be hard for you, but it's important for you to learn to say no, even to a friend.

An I CAN Girl Speaks Up to Parents

My parents used to worry that I had social problems. They thought that I was too shy. It's true that I'm afraid to speak up sometimes, particularly in school, but I'm not at all quiet around family and friends. My mom wanted me to have friends over to play every weekend, and that's where I thought she was wrong. I do have friends in school and sometimes I like them to come over. But most of the time I'm just happy playing with my sisters or by myself. No one seemed to believe me, though.

Finally I decided it was time to try to explain this to my mom. I said, "Mom, I'm just not as social as Jessica or Angie. (Those are my sisters.) When I read or draw, I'm happy to be alone. I play soccer, I love Scouts, and I'm with plenty of friends at school, but I'd rather just have my weekends with my family or alone instead of having friends over. I hope you understand."

She said she did, and she even admitted that she was not all that social when she was my age. Wow—what a relief! Time to be alone is what I really wanted. I'm glad I wasn't shy about speaking up to my mom. I didn't think she'd understand, but she did.—Ali

Overcoming Shyness and Stage Fright

Sandra Day O'Connor, the first woman ever appointed to the U.S. Supreme Court, is one of many successful women who overcame her childhood shyness. Thanks to practice, and the encouragement of a dramatic arts teacher, she now speaks up all the time! "Under my teacher's direction, I learned to get up in front of people and say things," says Justice O'Connor. "It is something that has helped me the rest of my life."

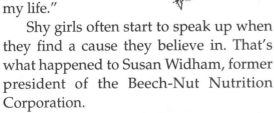

Shy girls often start to speak up when they find a cause they believe in. That's what happened to Susan Widham, former president of the Beech-Nut Nutrition Corporation.

When Susan first started working for Beech-Nut, the company wasn't doing well. As a young mom with a baby at home, Susan believed in the importance of healthy baby food. One day she saw her boss at the supermarket. Despite her shyness, Susan stopped him in the aisle and offered her ideas for Beech-Nut's baby food line. Before she knew it, Susan was working in the baby food department. The line became successful . . . and Susan soon became Beech-Nut's first female president!

Many of the *See Jane Win* women—especially those who wound up with careers in law, politics, or media—participated in student government, theater, speech contests, or debate teams when they were growing up. This helped them build their confidence and practice their speaking skills while they were kids.

Take television news anchor Jane Pauley, for example. When she didn't make her high school's cheerleading squad, she was discouraged. Then the school's debate coach convinced her to try out for the debate team. She became such a strong debater that kids on opposing teams dreaded competing against her. The confidence she gained from these experiences steered her toward a career in TV.

Do you see yourself in the spotlight someday? Massachusetts district attorney Martha Coakley realized in middle school that she had a real talent for speaking out, but other women didn't feel comfortable sharing their opinions in a group until they were older. Tamara Minick-Scokalo, a marketing director for Proctor & Gamble, had no problem giving a speech, singing, or even playing the lead in the school play as a teenager. But when she didn't have words to memorize in advance, she'd freeze. At times she'd get so scared trying to talk up in a group that she'd faint! But the more she practiced, the better she became.

You *can* teach yourself to overcome shyness and stage fright. Here's the trick: Be more interested in what you're speaking about than in what other people think of you—or what they think of what you say. If you focus on what they're thinking, how can you pay attention to the ideas you're expressing? And if you worry too much about whether what you're saying is right or wrong, you can hardly concentrate on the words you're using to say what's on your mind!

In some ways, not speaking up is like hiding yourself from others. Maybe you're always thinking ahead to what you're going to say and then are too afraid to say it. But don't do this type of disappearing act! You may feel safer not talking, but hiding won't make people like you better. They can't get to know you that way! Be yourself and just trust that others will accept you for who you are. And if they don't, let that be their problem, not yours.

Even if you'll always be a quiet person, you can develop the social confidence to speak up when you have a reason to. It sure beats appearing to agree with something you don't agree with, or going along with something you think is wrong! Once you start talking, the worst that can happen is that someone will disagree or try to correct you. That isn't so terrible. It happens to everyone—even the most outgoing kids in class—all the time. So, go ahead: Let your I CAN girl voice be heard!

An I CAN Girl Speaks Up to Teachers

My name is LaKeisha. I love to sing and we were getting ready for the spring concert. One song on the program was "Pharaoh, Pharaoh, He's Our Man." I was enjoying singing this song when I started to pay attention to the words. I kept thinking that Pharaoh's not my man because he didn't let the Hebrew slaves go. There are kids in my class whose great-grandparents were slaves. It just didn't feel right to sing that song. I talked to my friend about it and she agreed with me.

That night, I talked to my mom about my problem. I asked her if I should ask my teacher if we could sing a different song. She encouraged me to talk to my teacher but warned me that the teacher might say no. I wanted to do it anyway.

The next day, my friend came with me to talk to my music teacher. I did the talking, but I was glad my friend was at my side. I was very polite and explained my worry. My teacher looked surprised. She said she hadn't quite thought about it that way, that she'd think about it some more, but for now we were going to sing it anyway. She did tell me that I didn't have to sing it if I didn't want to. I was disappointed.

A week later, I was surprised. She told us we wouldn't sing about Pharaoh and she taught us "Go Down Moses" instead. I liked singing "Let my people go." I'm glad I had the courage to speak up. Even kids can make a difference.

And the Survey Says:
Of everyone interviewed in the *See Jane Win* study, lawyers were the earliest talkers. Women in media, especially TV and radio, came in second place.

Learning to Speak Out

Still feel hesitant about being in the spotlight? Here are some tips that may help you become more outgoing over time:

When you talk too little: If you're afraid to speak up in class or in a group because you may say something wrong, keep a small note pad on which you write the responses that you would have given. Count the number of times others express thoughts like yours. Count the number of times that your answers would have been correct if you'd said them out loud. Then take a chance and speak up when you're afraid. Start by doing this at least once a day. After a week, start doing this at least twice a day. The teacher, your friends—and you—will soon start to see how smart you are and how much you really know.

When you talk too much: If you ever feel that others don't listen when you're talking, or think they see you as a show-off, find ways to express yourself in fewer words. Before you raise your hand, take a minute to organize your thinking, either in your head or on paper. Others will be impressed when you make your points clearly and briefly. Plus you'll feel tuned in instead of tuned out!

Show what you don't know: Never be afraid to ask questions. Otherwise how will you ever find out what you don't know? Teachers, parents, classmates, and others will be glad to add to your knowledge. And those with similar questions who were afraid to speak up will be really glad that you did. But don't make the mistake of asking silly questions just to get attention. That really turns people off.

Organize a poetry or drama club: Performing is good practice for speaking out in front of a group. As Tamara Minick-Scokalo learned, performing skits or reading poems is easier than giving speeches because the words you're saying have already been written down. If you like, serve refreshments at your poetry or drama club meetings. Turning these events into parties takes the stress away from being out front.

Hold a great debate: In a debate, two teams each argue a different side of an issue. The topics can range from politics to school rules to dress codes. In addition to providing practice in public speaking, debates also help you see that sometimes people aren't right or wrong but just have different opinions.

Run for student council or class office: If you have an interest in politics and there's a student government in your school, run for a position. Create a speech explaining what you would do as a leader, and come up with an original campaign slogan. Even if you don't win, you'll learn a lot, and the experience may give you the confidence to try again later on.

Everything I've done that led me on the path to being chief was motivated by passion and by the issues. I saw needs and felt moved to try to do something about them. For example, I became director of the Cherokee Nation's Community Development Department because some of our people really needed housing, so I felt I could do something about that. Even if I'd lacked the self-confidence to run for office, my feelings about the issues at hand would have overcome that because I felt so strongly about them.

–Wilma P. Mankiller, former Principal Chief, Cherokee Nation

I had a few good friends [as a kid], but I was mainly a loner. I was sure it was all my fault that I didn't have more friends. I was prickly and not easy to get along with, and I learned to enjoy being alone and depending on myself. I grew up on a farm and loved being with the animals and taking walks in the woods. I still do. Getting away from people is perhaps the best way to get perspective on the day again.

–Christine Todd Whitman, Administrator, U.S. Environmental Protection Agency; Former Governor of New Jersey

> *I wasn't the prettiest or the most popular. I was very gawky, with curly dark hair that I went out of my way to iron and straighten at a time when having straight blond hair was in. But I was very active in student government and Jewish youth groups. I was committed to standing up for what I believed in.*
>
> **–Shelley Berkley, U.S. Congresswoman from Nevada**

And the Survey Says:
The successful women in *See Jane Win* found most of their friends among kids who worked hard in school and were involved in positive extracurricular activities.

A Different Kind of Leadership

Leadership is another type of social intelligence that can serve you well in your lifetime. Some girls naturally feel comfortable about taking charge. If you're one of them, consider yourself fortunate. But if you're not, chances are you still have good ideas, ideas that are worth sharing. Maybe your strength comes from working behind the scenes, developing a quieter leadership style.

That's the way Merle Waxman, associate dean at Yale Medical School, is. She describes herself not as a take-charge kind of person but as a make-things-happen-smoothly type. Rather than take the lead in the many school service groups she participated in as a kid, Merle preferred a cooperative approach to organizing. This cooperative leadership style still works for her today as she helps professors and students resolve their problems and complaints.

> *The most important thing that anybody can bring to leadership is a positive attitude. People don't want to follow leaders who are whiny or negative, or who give up. If you're forward-thinking and have a positive attitude, you see barriers as challenges. Native American girls must step up to lead in good and positive ways.*
>
> **–Wilma P. Mankiller, former Principal Chief, Cherokee Nation**

How about you? Are you more comfortable in or out of the limelight? Either way—whether it's organizing a recycling drive, taking your turn running a family meeting, or running for student council— you can find a leadership style that suits you.

Tips for How You Can Improve Your Social Intelligence

- Be your own best friend. Make it a habit to take time for yourself.

- Know who your true friends are—and be a good friend in return.

- Treat others the way you want to be treated. Be as kind as you can be—but not to the point where you're not taking care of yourself.

- Don't label yourself or others. See all people as the unique individuals they are.

- Be independent! Don't give in to peer pressure. Always try to do the right thing.

- If others pick on you, do your best to ignore it. But if things don't get better, or you come across a problem that's too big for you to handle, find an adult you trust and get help.

- Speak up when you have something to say.

- Reach out and get to know others. You won't be sorry that you did.

Chapter 5

Tuning in to Your Talents

local library, or win a post on your school's student council.

And the Survey Says:
When the *See Jane Win* women were asked about their most positive childhood experiences, "winning a competition" was the most frequently mentioned experience.

No one is a winner or a loser all the time. You can hit a softball out of a ballpark one inning and then strike out your next time at bat. Or you may find yourself full of confidence as you rehearse for a piano recital but then frozen by stage fright during the actual event.

But if you succeed at something often, why not challenge yourself by entering a competition? It's fun to watch yourself improve. And you'll build confidence and learn discipline if you set out to achieve something difficult, maybe even something you once thought you couldn't do. Maybe you'll get a medal, a certificate of achievement, a trophy, or some other honor. Maybe you'll become a spelling bee or bowling league champ, hear a song you wrote performed at a school assembly, see your artwork on display at the

But achievement doesn't always mean competition, and you don't need awards to prove your talent. You may pride yourself on your woodworking, hiking, baking, stamp collecting, kite making, or ability to care for animals. You may never win or even participate in a contest. But you still can be proud of what you do.

If you know a lot about one thing, it's easy to see where your strengths lie. But what if you'd like to achieve in several areas? Can you do this without spreading yourself too thin? Or what if you don't

think you have any special skills or talents? Then think again! You may just need to experiment a bit to find them.

Each time you try a new activity you find out more about yourself, about your talents and your interests—and about new interests that you may want to pursue. So instead of worrying about what you're *not* good at, take a chance and try something new!

> *A major milestone for me was winning a speaking tournament at Ball State University. Before that, I didn't know the feeling of being number one. I really liked it. I kept at it for three years, ultimately becoming a state champion and competing in the national tournament.*
>
> **–Jane Pauley, Television News Anchor**

> *I was a joiner. You name it, I was a member. The experience of joining a club or trying out for the orchestra, entering a competition, or volunteering was invaluable. I even ran for student council. I didn't win, but I always learned something about myself. I not only met different people, I learned the importance of taking a risk, of being responsible, and of developing good people skills—all things that I still use today.*
>
> **–Judy Galbraith, Founder and President, Free Spirit Publishing Inc.**

Create Your Own Interest Inventory

Even if you already have hobbies or interests, an **Interest Inventory** can help you look at the activities you do in a new way. It can also help you find new things to try. Here's how to fill it out:

1. **Make a photocopy of the Interest Inventory Chart on page 59. In the first column, Activity, list the activities that you're already involved in.** (This Activity List may give you some ideas.)

Activity List

Aerobics
Art
Band/orchestra
Bicycle riding
Cheerleading
Choir/chorus
Computer programming
Dancing
Debate
Drama
Email/instant messaging
Foreign language
Gymnastics
Hiking/camping
Horseback riding
Jogging
Martial arts
Nature study
Painting
Playing a musical instrument
Playing a sport

Playing board games
Reading
Religious activities
Science projects
Scouts
Seeing movies
Singing
Solving puzzles
Spending time alone
Stamp/coin collecting
Student government
Surfing the Internet
Talking on the phone
Volunteer work
Watching a sport
Watching TV
Woodworking
Writing
Yoga

2. **In the second column of your chart, How I Feel About It, give each of the activities you listed one of these five ratings:**

> 5 - I absolutely love this activity.

> 4 - I like this activity a lot.

> 3 - This activity is pretty fun.

> 2 - This activity is a little boring.

> 1 - I don't like this activity at all.

3. **In the third column of your chart, My Talent/Skill Level, rate your skill in each of the activities:**

> 5 - I'm better at this activity than almost anyone I know.

> 4 - I'm far above average in this activity but not at the top.

> 3 - I'm pretty good at this activity.

> 2 - I think I'm below average in this activity.

> 1 - I'm really bad at this activity.

If this column doesn't apply to some activities you do, such as watching TV or spending time alone, simply write N/A (not applicable) in that space.

4. **In the last column, What I Get from It, list the benefits you get from each activity. For example, an activity may be creative, social, relaxing, challenging, or help you to keep fit. It might also help you develop responsibility or good people skills, or improve your tolerance for risk-taking. Write as many benefits for each activity as you feel apply.**

My Interest Inventory Chart

Activity	How I Feel About It (Rate 1–5)	My Talent/ Skill Level (Rate 1–5)	What I Get from It

Analyzing Your Interest Inventory

When you're ready, take a closer look at the Interest Inventory you created. In general, do you like the activities that you're best at? Or do you tend to prefer activities that are relaxing or that present a challenge? Are your favorite activities things you do alone or do they usually involve other people? Do they demand special athletic, artistic, or computer skills? What else do they have in common?

Now look at the following chart and compare the activities you like best with the ones that women in various careers preferred when they were kids.

Most Frequent Activities of SEE JANE WIN Women When They Were Girls, According to Career*

Artists
Art
Drama
Outdoors/
environment
Reading
TV

Business
Drama
Reading
Scouts
Sports
Student government
Writing

Doctors
Foreign language
Music
Outdoors/
environmental
Reading
Science
Scouts
Spending time alone
Sports

Government
Cheerleading
Debate
Drama
Reading
Scouts
Spending time alone
Student government

Homemakers
Drama
Foreign language
Scouts
Spending time alone
Sports
TV

Lawyers
Debate
Drama
Foreign language
Music
Reading
Scouts
Spending time alone
Student government

Media (Radio and TV anchors, Authors, Reporters)
Art
Cheerleading
Dance
Drama
Music
Reading
Speech
Spending time alone
Sports
Student government
TV
Writing

Nurses
Art
Music
Reading
Science
Scouts
TV

Orchestral Musicians
Foreign language
Music
Reading
Spending time alone

Psychologists
Dance
Reading
Scouts
Spending time alone
Sports
Student government

Scientists
Foreign language
Music
Outdoors/
environmental
Reading
Science
Scouts
Spending time alone
Sports

Teachers
Drama
Music
Reading
Scouts
Sports
Student government

*Activities are listed in alphabetical order, not by importance. Volunteering and community service were not on the original checklist that the *See Jane Win* women filled out, but many said that they also valued community service as girls. Most continue to volunteer today.

There are no right or wrong answers on the Interest Inventory. But your responses may tell you something about yourself—and even about the type of career that might suit you best. For example, if you're very social, you may want to do something that allows you to work with large groups of people. Careers such as teaching, politics, sales, marketing, or media (television, radio, or newspaper and magazine reporting) might be right for you. If you're less social or like being by yourself, you might enjoy a career that allows you to work alone or with one or two people at a time. A career as a scientist, artist, accountant, computer programmer, doctor, or nurse might suit you. If you're about average in your sociability, any of these careers might work for you.

As you can see from the chart, women in many fields enjoyed some of the activities, like reading, music, scouting, and spending time alone. Other activities interested fewer people. The people most interested in science, for example, became doctors, nurses, and scientists.

Your list probably won't match the list under any of the careers exactly. These lists were made by compiling the activities of many women in each field. So no woman was actually involved in all of the activities listed in a particular column. But if your list looks a bit like any of them, you may want to explore that as a possible career direction. Or if you already have a career in mind, see if there are activities listed under it that you've never tried. You may want to find out more about them.

And the Survey Says:
More than three-fourths of all the *See Jane Win* women participated in an all-girls Scout group or sports activity or went to an all-girls school at some point during their childhood.

Just Us Girls

As you review your list of activities, see if any of them are for girls only. If not, think about signing up for something that is— an activity like Girls Scouts, Girls Inc., or an all-girls team sport. Dr. Victoria Brady*, an orthopedic surgeon who describes herself as having been "a spindly kid" found that, with encouragement from a demanding coach, she was able to make the girls' swimming team at her school. "I grew stronger, and it gave me a place to belong," she says, looking back fondly on it.

Marilyn Carlson Nelson and Charlotte Otto, both corporate executives, gained a lot from their all-girl groups also. Each found that the years they spent in Girl Scouts were great training for the business world. "Scouting taught me teamwork and was the center of my social existence," Charlotte remembers. "In my work today, I take great pride in building a strong team of women, and that came directly from my Girl Scout activities."

Many successful women say that they felt more confident as kids when boys weren't around. Sometimes this was because boys dominated their co-ed groups (intentionally or not), taking the leadership away from girls. Some girls also felt more self-conscious with the guys, or more focused on trying to attract or impress them than on mastering the skills they were there to learn.

> *The values I see in myself today come from my friends of the same sex. In ninth grade, I met my friends for life. We called ourselves the Swift Six, and those friends did wonders for my self-confidence. The six of us still get together every year and float down the river on a rubber raft.*
>
> **–Barbara Cubin, U.S. Congresswoman from Wyoming**

It's important for boys and girls to learn how to get along, and as long as everyone is respectful of one another co-ed activities can be a great thing. But sometimes an all-girl group is just what you need to build confidence and make the most of your I CAN girl leadership skills.

Expanding Your Interest Horizons

What if you're not crazy about most of the activities on your list? What if you don't do much of anything now except maybe watch television, play computer games, or put together jigsaw puzzles? What if you've noticed that there's a theme to your Interest Inventory—like art, sports, or science-related activities—and you're ready to try something new? Then follow these five steps to expand your horizons:

Look around: Ask your parents, teachers, friends, and neighbors to suggest activities for you to try. You might also visit your local Y, Boys and Girls Club, recreation or community center, or place of worship to find out what they offer. Local newspapers, school bulletin boards, community Internet sites, and newsletters are also good places to look for ideas.

Make a list: Write down any and all activities that sound interesting to you. Don't worry if your list is long. The next steps will help you narrow it down.

Be practical: Some activities are expensive, or are located too far away for you to get to on your own. Go through your list considering each of these four factors for each activity:

- Age-range for the activity

- Cost, including any materials or uniforms you may need

- Distance from your home and means of transportation

- Time investment or other sacrifices the activity may demand

Then cross out anything that seems unrealistic. If an activity interests you but you're not sure it's realistic, discuss it with a parent. Could someone give you a ride? Can your family afford it or can you find a way to raise money for it? Or is there another way to participate in this type of activity? (For example, you don't need special clothes or a fancy gym to exercise. Borrow a videotape from your local library and make time at home to follow along.) If it's not realistic, take it off the list for now. If the interest stays with you, you can always make trying it later one of your goals.

Balance out your activities: If you already know how to play piano, guitar, drums, flute, and clarinet, consider putting off lessons in oboe and trombone. The same holds true if the activities on

your Inventory are all related to computers, sports, art, or any other single topic. Experience something new!

Do some research: If your list is still too long, maybe you can sit in and observe one or more of the activities that you're considering. While you're there, talk to kids who are involved in the program to find what they like about it and what they don't. When you make your final decision, don't worry about how good you think you'll be at something. You won't know that until you try!

You may not find an activity right away that you feel passionate about—one that you would score a 5 in your How I Feel About It column. It takes some people a long time to find an interest that strikes such a strong chord. So have patience. In the meantime, enjoy trying a variety of activities. They'll help you become more interesting, knowledgeable, and well rounded.

Hitting a Wall

As you work to discover what your strengths and interests are, and as you challenge yourself to get better, you'll have to learn perseverance—the ability not to give up, even when things get really tough. When something becomes difficult, don't automatically assume that you don't have a talent for it. Some skills are harder to master than others.

Imagine you're walking along a road and come to a huge wall that's blocking your way. It will take a lot of effort to get to the other side. But once you've made up your mind to do it, then the only question is how! If you stick with an activity long enough, you're bound to come to something like that wall—something that requires plenty of effort and perseverance. People refer to this as "hitting a wall" because it feels like you can't get past it. When you hit a wall in music,

dance, sports, or a school subject, you may feel like turning around and quitting. Don't! Be persistent and make the extra effort. Ask someone to give you a boost. Or grab a rope and start climbing. Invent new tools to help you scale the wall. Dig a tunnel under it if you have to!

The person who gives you a boost could be a parent, a teacher, or a classmate. But you need to help yourself, too.

When New Jersey Assemblywoman Mary Previte lost her left hand on a revolving saw at age fourteen, she hit wall after wall as she learned how to do basic tasks with one hand—tie her shoelaces, type, wash the dishes. Both of her parents encouraged her to persevere. They refused to let her get away with saying "I can't." "Yes, you can," they insisted.

Today Mary does just about everything that other people need two hands to do. She makes quilts, hangs wallpaper, drives a car, and has a very responsible job—all largely because her parents wouldn't allow her to give up, give in, or feel sorry for herself.

> *My dad believed in me. He said "Handicaps have nothing to do with the outside of a person. Handicaps are only on the inside."*
>
> **—Mary Previte,
> Assemblywoman, New Jersey**

When she was learning to play the oboe as a kid, environmental engineer Teresa Culver hit many walls. She found that it helped to break hard musical passages into smaller parts. She practiced each section over and over until she got it right. Then, when she was ready, she put them together. Later, in her college math and engineering courses, she used the same strategy, breaking tough assignments into smaller parts.

An I CAN Girl Perseveres

My name is Sara and I want to tell you how I learned to swim. I'm the youngest of four kids and my brothers and sisters were good swimmers. I loved the water, too, but I couldn't swim. Mom thought that was dangerous, so she signed me up for swimming lessons. I passed the Beginner's test right away and moved into Advanced Beginners where you put your head in the water and learn how to breathe while you're swimming. I'm not that coordinated, so I had a hard time with this.

At the end of the course, they tested us. I failed the test. That wasn't so bad, because some of the other kids failed, too. Mom suggested I take the class again. I did, but I still couldn't get it right. I failed the test again, and this time the other kids passed. I felt like a dork. I cried a little, but Mom said I shouldn't get discouraged. If I kept practicing I'd surely get it.

When I failed the third, fourth, and fifth time I didn't cry, but I think my mom felt like crying. She didn't, but I could tell she felt bad for me. I thought I was getting better and the teacher told me she could see my improvement. That encouraged me a little, so I just said, "I CAN" and didn't quit.

Can you believe I had to take that class eight times before I finally passed the test? I guess I'm a slow learner in some ways. Once I passed, I became a good swimmer. I kept taking more advanced classes and I passed those tests the first time. I finally caught on. I like swimming now and I can swim a mile. I'm glad I didn't give up.

Sometimes it's hard to find a way over the wall, but keep practicing and be persistent. The more you do something— like hit a baseball, paint pictures, or turn cartwheels—the better at it you become. When you feel you just can't do it anymore, promise yourself a reward when you're done. Say to yourself, "After I memorize my lines for the first act of the school play, I'll take a break and call a friend," or "As soon as I've done my dance routine three times in a row without a mistake, I'll treat myself to ice cream."

Remember that it's okay to ask for help when you need it. Maybe a friend, coach, classmate, or family member can read along and double-check you as you learn those lines for the play, or observe and offer encouragement while you practice your dance routine. But if you don't ask for help, the people who could give you a hand might not even notice that you're struggling!

If you're still discouraged, think back to how you played piano a year ago or to the basketball skills you had at the beginning of the season. Recognizing your progress can help you persevere.

Taking the Heat When You Compete

Have you ever met someone who enjoyed losing? Probably not. But unless you accept the possibility of losing, you'll never take the risks required to be a winner! The reality is that most people lose at least as many times as they win, so it's important not to let losing make you feel like a loser. Sure, you'll feel disappointed at times. Everyone does. But remember that while winning builds confidence, losing develops your strength of character.

Suppose you just joined the track team and you're competing against kids who have been running for a long time. You may fall behind a lot at the beginning. But if you keep at it, eventually you'll start to catch up as you become stronger and faster. In the meantime (hopefully!) you'll be having a good time.

It may not be easy to keep your I CAN attitude going while you're learning. But stay focused on your own performance. Tell yourself, "Maybe I'm not as skilled or as fast as my friends are, but I'm better than I was last week." Seeing how far you've progressed can give you the confidence you need to keep at it. Look at it this way: Whenever you run, swim, or calculate math faster or better than you did yesterday, you're experiencing the thrill of winning. And even when you don't beat yesterday's record, competing against yourself allows you to stretch your abilities—without feeling too much pressure. If it helps, keep repeating "I can do it! I can do it! I can do it!" over and over to yourself as you keep trying. Say something often enough and you just may start to believe it!

How can you learn to deal with the times you don't win? Becoming a good loser takes practice. One way to do this is to invite a friend to join you for some board or card games. Since luck has a lot to do with many of these, try not to take them too seriously. You'll win some and

you'll lose some. And so will your opponents. You might even challenge each other to see who can be the more gracious loser.

You could also join a team of some sort—sports, chess, debate, academic competition. When your team loses—and teams do lose sometimes—you won't be alone in your disappointment. And, when you win, you won't be alone in winning either! You'll see the different ways that people on the team react to winning and losing. And you'll discover that, one way or another, everyone gets through it.

> *I was very active in sports. I set records in track and field. At one track meet, I got four first-place ribbons and one second. I went home sobbing my eyes out because of the second-place ribbon. My father was so mad at me because I didn't appreciate what I'd won, only what I'd lost. That was a valuable lesson in perspective.*
>
> **–Barbara Cubin, U.S. Congresswoman from Wyoming**

The next time you're at a game, compare the actions of the good and bad sports. Do the kids who lose and throw their gloves down or storm off the field impress you? Or do you have more respect for the ones who come over and shake their opponents' hands? Once you see how both look from the stands, it may be easier to do the right thing yourself.

Between high school and college, I was an exchange student in Norway, living with a family where the two boys were national hiking and track champions. The whole family was athletic and went cross-country skiing several times a week. I learned that if I wanted to go cross-country skiing, I didn't actually have to be good at it, only enjoy it.

–Cady Coleman, NASA Astronaut

Is It Ever Okay to Be a Quitter?

Business executive Tamara Minick-Scokalo went to twelve to fifteen hours of ballet class every week while she was growing up. She loved it and even dreamed of becoming a prima ballerina. But at some point she had to accept that she was not one of the top dancers in her class. Eventually she decided to put her energies into other activities and to set those old dreams aside. "I learned that life is a series of trade-offs," she says. "By the time I made my decision, I knew what I was trading, and that the path I had selected was the one I wanted."

Even if you're great at handling competition, you may still not want to stick with every activity you try, or climb every wall blocking your way. You may find that an activity is no longer fun, or too painful, or just not worth it. If that happens, it may be time to leave it behind and do something else. That's not giving up. That's making choices!

If you've persevered for a fair amount of time—stayed on a team until the end of the season, for example—and given an activity your best shot, you may eventually decide that it's just not right for you, or that the amount of effort you'd have to put into it isn't worth it. Before you make that decision, though, ask yourself these questions:

- How hard have I worked to achieve this goal? What have I gotten for my efforts?

- What will I be giving up if I leave now? Am I sure the trade-offs are worth it?

- Am I running away from a challenge or will I be using my new free time in a better, more balanced way?

- Will I feel like a quitter if I stop now?

- Is there something else that I might like to put my energies into instead? Do I know what that is and am I ready to pursue it?

Only you can determine whether to move on or keep trying. But before you move on, be sure that you've at least *tried* to climb the wall. Then think through your decision, consider the trade-offs, and have confidence in your instincts. As long as you've weighed the arguments on both sides, you have no reason to second-guess your decision.

Cheaters Never Win

Do you ever cheat, or feel tempted to? Oh, come on now—you can admit it! Maybe you think it's no big deal to move a playing piece ahead a few spaces on a board game when your opponent isn't looking, or copy another kid's test paper, or claim a softball has gone foul when it hasn't.

Competition can put pressure on kids to break the rules and do things that they know are wrong. Some try to justify themselves by saying things like, "It's no big deal. All the kids copy. We're just doing each other a favor."

You know there's a big difference between helping out others and cheating. And even if lots of people do it, it's still wrong. That's what really matters! Breaking the rules in all of these cases is dishonest, and it's unfair to the people who didn't cheat. It's also unfair to you. It makes others look bad when they should

have won and makes you seem like a winner when you really aren't. In school, it may even trick a teacher into thinking you know things that you really don't.

I remember once, during a test, I couldn't help but notice the girl who sat in front of me. She kept pushing her sleeve up and down while we were taking our science test. I couldn't imagine what she was doing and it was distracting. Later, I asked her if there was something wrong with her arm. She laughed as she pulled up her sleeve to show me an arm full of small printing. She had neatly written science definitions on her arm. It seemed funny to me because it must have taken her hours to print all that information. If she had studied for half that time, I was sure she would have earned an A. I always thought less of her afterward and wondered why she thought she had to cheat.

Back when your parents were kids, there was a chant that went "Cheaters never prosper." It's true. Not only are cheaters being dishonest, they miss out on the satisfaction of learning and improving their skills. And if they get caught (which they often do), their teachers, parents, classmates, and friends will have a hard time trusting them again. So any way you look at it, in the long run cheaters really are the losers.

I CAN!

Tips for How You Can
Develop New Interests and Talents

- Keep an open mind about new activities—even if no one else you know does them and even if your friends don't think they're cool.

- Many new activities feel hard at first, so don't give up after your first try.

- Practice your activity a little each day.

- Once you start an activity, finish at least one season. Don't drop out in the middle.

- Make getting to know new kids part of the fun of trying something new.

- Don't try too many new activities at once; don't spread yourself too thin.

- If you're already involved in too many activities, don't add any new ones until you figure out which ones to drop.

- Look for ways that the activities you enjoy are alike. Find new activities that combine your interests, new experiences, and fun.

- Accept that competition is a part of life and that most things worth doing take a lot of perseverance and effort.

- Don't cheat yourself by being a cheater.

- Always remain enthusiastic!

Exploring the World

In social studies classes, you've probably learned about Marco Polo, Christopher Columbus, Ferdinand Magellan, and

those other (typically male) Old-World explorers who endured great hardships to travel beyond their familiar worlds. But every I CAN girl can also become an explorer whenever she visits places that are new to her.

Farm life, for example, can be an eye-opening adventure if you live in the suburbs. A fishing-village will be a new experience to most city kids. And if you're used to small-town living, your first visit to a large city will probably open up a very different world to you.

Adventures Close to Home

Don't forget that there are also plenty of interesting places to discover right in your own neighborhood. You probably pass some of them every day, without realizing that adventures await you inside. Check with your town's Chamber of Commerce, if it has one. They can tell you about fun local things to do. Read a community newspaper or the newspaper in the largest city near you—especially the entertainment section of the Friday edition—for plays, museums, art exhibits, concerts, and other special events. Some of these may be expensive but some will be free or inexpensive.

> *My dad would save up his vacation time so we could all (I had five sisters and brothers) pile into the family station wagon and drive to the national parks to camp and hike for five weeks. I grew up loving nature because our vacations were enriched with learning about the biology and geology of the areas we visited.*
>
> **–Teresa Culver, Environmental Engineer**

> *My mother used to take me places every Sunday. We didn't have money to travel far, but she took me to museums, and we went to Washington, D.C. Those trips compensated for what I couldn't learn from reading, because I had a reading disability. I discovered the joy of learning and developed great curiosity. My mother has her own natural curiosity, and although she is ninety-one we continue to go to museums together.*
>
> **–Martha Lindner, Attorney**

And the Survey Says:
When the *See Jane Win* women were asked about their most positive experiences in childhood, "travel" was indicated second most frequently.

The Internet and the first few pages of your telephone directory can also tell you about interesting places nearby. An adult can show you how to find what you're looking for when you're using each of these.

Close-to-home adventures can expand your worldview almost as much as travel. For example, the first time you visit an art museum, a facility for the elderly, or even stay over at a friend's home—especially a friend who comes from a culture or background that's different from yours—you'll find out things that you never knew.

When she was growing up, business executive Connie Matsui traveled between two cultures every day without even stepping outside. That's because Connie's Japanese-American parents worked for and lived with a non-Asian family. The two families shared and compared their cultures, holidays, traditions, foods, music, art, and more.

Planning Ahead

To get the most out of any new experience, take the same approach that a journalist or detective would—be curious, do research, and ask a lot of questions. The more you plan ahead, the better. For example, if your family is going to take a vacation or visit a relative in another town, study maps with your mom or dad to find out the names of historic landmarks and other places you might see. Then use your local library and the Internet to collect interesting information about these places. You can also write to the Chambers of Commerce of the towns and cities you'll be visiting, or stop by a travel agency, and ask if they can give you brochures about these places.

If your family has plans to stop at a zoo, museum, or national park, find out more about it. Research what it's best known for and make sure to check out the highlights while you're there. Arrange your information in a file folder and take it with you on the trip so you can share it with your family.

You can use the same method to explore "dream destinations" you'd like to visit. If you're curious about the glaciers of

Iceland or the coral reefs of Australia, collect information about them. Then, when you actually do get to go there someday, you'll be all set to explore!

Collecting Photographs and Memories

A journalist or detective would probably carry a camera, camcorder, tape recorder, or journal, and you may want to do the same thing. Any of these can help you to capture the sights, sounds, and memories of your trip. Use the journal to keep a daily record of what happens. If you're taking pictures, you can also use the journal to record when, where, and why you chose to snap each shot.

If you prefer to talk rather than write, use the tape recorder to create a journal. You can also record unusual sounds or interview the people you are traveling with or meet. If you hear talks by tour guides or park rangers, ask if you can record these. Each time you replay the tape, you'll probably notice something you missed before.

When you can, pick up a postcard, dried leaf, interesting stone or shell, or some other small souvenir. Along with your journal, photos, and tape recordings, they will be a great record of your adventure, which you can share with friends, family, teachers, and classmates. If you like, you can create a scrapbook or memory box of all the items you've collected. You may want to bring your treasures into school as part of a report when you study a related topic.

Getting There Is Half the Fun . . . Or It Can Be, Anyway

There are probably a variety of ways to get to wherever you're going—from cars and airplanes to trains, buses, boats, bicycles, horse-drawn carriages, or your own two feet! The method will, in part, depend on how far you're going and what part of the world it's in. However you get there, and whether you're part of a family, a group, or on your own, it helps to know what to expect. That way you can be prepared for the trip as well as the destination. These tips can help:

If you're traveling by airplane . . . try to get a window seat (or at least take turns at it with your traveling buddies). That way, if the weather is clear, you can see how cars, houses, mountains, lakes, and rivers look from above. Bring along a book or CD player to keep you busy. And ask the airline attendant for a pillow and blanket. These are nice to have in case you want to doze off for a while.

If you're flying alone . . . airlines will refer to you as a UM, or unaccompanied minor. The flight attendant will probably stop by your seat every once in a while to ask how you are. He or she will also be there at the end of the flight to make sure that the people who should be picking you up do. In the meantime, stay busy reading a good book, watching a movie, or looking out the window. You'll be amazed at how quickly the time will "fly" by!

If you're traveling by car or bus . . . This can be quite an adventure, too, but keep your sense of humor handy, since being cooped up with a group of people can get tiring after a while. Bring a CD or tape player and listen to music or books on tape. Tell jokes, riddles, or stories if you can think of any good ones. Or invite other passengers (if you're in a car) to join you in a sing-along.

You can also try to interest others in games that will keep everyone looking out the window. For example, in I Spy, players take turns naming things that others have to find along the way. In License Plate, the players write down the names of states and provinces on any license plates that they see. The winner is the one with the longest list of names at the end of the game. You might also try to follow your route on a map. That way you'll know what you're passing, and how much farther you have to go. If there's time, ask if you can stop at monument signs. And make the most of any snack and bathroom breaks that you take. Do some stretches when you get out of the car or off the bus. They'll feel really good!

Every summer, my parents took us to visit a different national park. We saw them all, except for Acadia National Park in Maine. We would stop and read every single monument sign. If I fell asleep in the car, my mom would wake me to look at the view or a sign because I might never be in this special place again. To this day I cannot pass a monument or sign without stopping and reading every detail.

—Laurie Mitchell, Teacher

Meeting New People

Whenever you travel, there's always the chance of meeting new people. But before you start questioning strangers, check with the adult you're traveling with for help figuring out who it's safe to talk to and who may feel like talking to you.

Need a good icebreaker? Ask questions that will help you find out how other people's lives are like yours . . . and how they aren't. (See the suggestions on page 74 for ideas.) Don't just fire question after question, however. Listen to the responses and share some things about yourself also. Before you know it, you may have a new friend!

If you're in another country, or an area where your own language isn't spoken, you can still try making contact. See if you can come up with a friendly invented sign language, combined with words and phrases from the other person's language if you know any. You won't be able to carry on a long conversation, but you're likely to at least get a smile.

Of course, it's always important to be sensitive to other people and their differences. It's actually great that people don't all live the same way. Try to learn from others and let them learn from you. Perhaps you'll even find out about games, styles of music, or ways of doing things that you'd like to try. The more you travel, the more you'll appreciate the similarities and differences among people in the world.

Need a Conversation Starter?

Here are some questions you can ask when you first meet other kids:

School: What's your school like? Are the classes big or small? Is it an all-boys or all-girls school, or is it co-ed? What's your favorite subject? Do you have field trips? Are the teachers strict or easy? Do you get homework? Do you have school parties? Are kids there nice or mean? Do you have special classes? Do you have more than one teacher? Do kids from all different backgrounds go to your school?

Family: Who do you live with? How many sisters, brothers, stepsisters, or stepbrothers do you have? How old are they? Do you see other relatives, like grandparents, aunts, uncles, or cousins often? Do you have a favorite relative? What do you like to do together? Do you ever fight with them? What's it like being an only child, or a member of a large family? Do you like it that way, or do you wish you had more or fewer kids in your home?

Home: Do you live in the city, suburbs, a small town, or the country? Do you live in an apartment building, a trailer, or a house? Do you have a backyard or some other open space to play? Is there lots of traffic? Can you walk places or do you take a car, bus, or train? Do you share a room with anyone? Are there other homes near you? Did you ever move, or have you lived there your whole life?

Friends: What do you and your friends like to do together? Are you into sports or outdoor stuff? Are you in any clubs? Do most of your friends go to the same school as you? Do you go to many parties? Do you have one best friend?

Music: What kind of music do you like? Is that kind of music popular with your friends? Do you sing or play an instrument? Are you in a band, orchestra, or choir? Do you like to dance? What kind of dancing do you do? What are the dances at your school like?

Being Away from Home

Whether you're going to camp, to stay with relatives, or on a trip with a youth group, if you're away from home for the first time you'll probably feel more independent than you used to. You may also get homesick, but if it's any consolation, you probably won't be the only one.

One way to combat homesickness is to write letters to friends and family back home, describing what you're doing and how you're feeling and asking how things are there. Not only can this help you feel better, it will also give you a reason to check the mailbox to see if anyone wrote back.

When I was fifteen, friends of my parents who lived in England and had no children said, "We'd love to have Tamara visit us for the summer." At first, I didn't want to go because I'd miss my friends, but I went anyway. That trip opened my eyes to the world. I wanted to understand different cultures and experience things I had never thought about before. I realized my world was bigger than the town I grew up in, and I wanted to be part of it.

–Tamara Minick-Scokalo, Marketing Director, Procter & Gamble

When homesickness washes over you, keep busy. Find someone to hang out with—a fellow camper or group member who's having similar feelings, or an older person you can talk with openly. If you're really homesick and can't seem to shake it, ask the adult if you can call your family. Sometimes just hearing a familiar voice is all you need.

Summer camp provided my first inspiration for becoming a pilot. It was there that I discovered my love of the outdoors. I gazed at the stars at night and became passionate about astronomy. I became interested in early American history by finding Indian arrowheads, too. The importance of cooperation combined with the adventurous spirit of those summers was perfect preparation for the military. There was a glider airfield near the camp. As I observed those gliders, they lured me toward the sky. I imagined that someday I, too, would fly.

–Eileen Collins, NASA Astronaut and Space Shuttle Commander

Paying for the Trip

Travel can be expensive. But I CAN girls have managed to earn part, or all, of their travel money if they want to go somewhere badly enough. For example, if you want to travel with a school, religious, community, or youth group, you might work together to hold a car wash, bake sale, raffle, or other fund-raiser. If you're planning a trip on your own, you can wash cars, mow lawns, or baby-sit the neighbors' kids. Show by your actions that the trip is important enough to you and, if they can, your mom or dad may be willing to chip in the extra dollars you need.

Many summer camps are expensive, but some aren't. And some—especially ones that focus on a special talent or interest, such as computers, creative writing, art, science, or baseball—often have scholarship programs that you may qualify for.

> In Senior Scouts, we made paper dogwoods that we sold at the local spring festival so we could attend Mystic Seaport Sailing School. I made them, I sold them, I earned my money, and I went to sailing school—all tangible results of my efforts.
>
> **—Charlotte Otto, Senior Vice-President and Global External Relations Officer, Procter & Gamble**

Stay-at-Home Travel

Sometimes, though, parents have to say no to even your most wonderful plans. They may be concerned about your safety or their finances, or they may expect you to be doing something else at the time. While you can certainly ask them to explain their reasons, you may, in the end, just have to accept what they say.

But there are plenty of cheap, easy, safe ways to travel that your parents aren't likely to object to. That's because, through books and your imagination, you can go anywhere in the world! Wildlife photographer Frances Bayless, for example, became fascinated by her teacher's descriptions of Antarctica—one of the coldest places on Earth. She could see it perfectly in her mind when she began reading about it. But she didn't actually get there until she was over sixty.

So, while you're waiting for permission or to raise the money, start planning. Think about the places that sound interesting, or the places where your own ancestors or your close friends' ancestors came from. Then read books, magazine articles, and encyclopedia entries, and see movies about the ones that interest you most.

Marva Collins, founder of Chicago's Marva Collins Preparatory School, kept a travel journal when she was younger. "I would say 'I visited Germany today, and I went to the Rhine River yesterday, and I went to Greece and saw the Acropolis,' all based on my reading. I would read books from all over the world and create imaginary friends in those countries."

Your friends in other lands don't have to be imaginary. Ask a teacher or some other adult to help you find a pen pal—either over the Internet or by mail. Learn about your new friend's part of the world and tell her or him about yours. Of course, you have to be careful about giving your name and address or email address to strangers, but as long as you follow your parent or teacher's safety guidelines, you should be fine.

> *On days when I couldn't go out or didn't feel like being around other kids,
> I'd get out the encyclopedias. I wouldn't read them cover to cover,
> but I'd skim through them, learning about states and countries
> and dreaming about going to these places.*
>
> **–Janice Huff, Meteorologist, NBC's TODAY, WEEKEND EDITION**

I CAN!

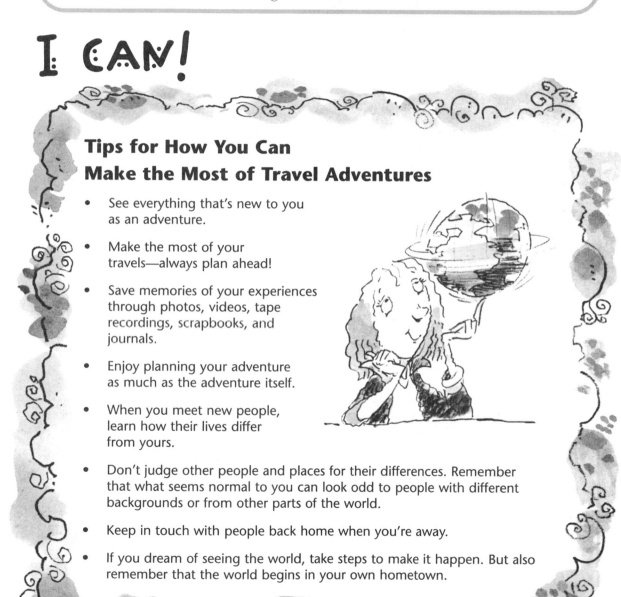

Tips for How You Can
Make the Most of Travel Adventures

- See everything that's new to you as an adventure.

- Make the most of your travels—always plan ahead!

- Save memories of your experiences through photos, videos, tape recordings, scrapbooks, and journals.

- Enjoy planning your adventure as much as the adventure itself.

- When you meet new people, learn how their lives differ from yours.

- Don't judge other people and places for their differences. Remember that what seems normal to you can look odd to people with different backgrounds or from other parts of the world.

- Keep in touch with people back home when you're away.

- If you dream of seeing the world, take steps to make it happen. But also remember that the world begins in your own hometown.

Chapter 7

When Things Change

Just when things are going pretty smoothly in your life, something happens: Your dad comes home and announces that your family is moving. Your parents tell you that they're getting a divorce. You break your leg and can't play the sports that are a huge part of your life. A parent, grandparent, or friend dies unexpectedly. Suddenly you feel that things just couldn't get any worse!

Major changes like these can be shocking . . . even if you were, up to that point, one of the most together kids around. But take heart: You have the strength to deal with whatever happens. How? By reaching *inside* yourself and *out* to others who can ride the waves of change with you. Remember that change is a part of life. As an I CAN girl, you CAN learn, grow, and sometimes enjoy yourself, even when things get turned upside down.

I grew up in Tacoma, Washington, surrounded by a tight-knit family and lots of friends. I went to an excellent junior high school with accelerated classes in science, math, English, and Spanish.

Then my father accepted a job transfer. I will never forget that first day in my new school, sitting in my old-fashioned desk, complete with runners and inkwells and fifty years of carved initials. The teachers were uninspiring, the classes boring, and the curriculum ancient. I remember weeping behind my books.

My new peers were also harder to understand. There was much more flirting, and the girls wore clothes that were totally out of date at my old school. I had just come from a big city, where there had been students of many backgrounds and races; here, there were no African-American or Latino kids. I felt like I had moved to a different planet.

–Susan Lemagie, M.D., Obstetrician-Gynecologist and Women's Health Activist

After my sophomore year, we moved to Florida. My parents were having some marriage and financial problems, and they decided to move in hopes of improving their lifestyle. That never came about. My mom raised us four kids alone and worked full time.

I was so mad about being in Florida that I was hard on everybody. But after the first six months, I settled down. I realized, "Okay, I'm going to make the best of this; I can't be miserable."

My algebra teacher was great, and he made me statistician for the wrestling team. I got very involved in school, had a very traditional senior year, went to the prom, and was active in homecoming. I was awarded the Most School Spirit award. What turned me around in Florida was that nobody gave up on me.

–Lisa Hayes-Taylor, Elementary School Teacher

But I Don't Want to Move!

You don't usually have a choice about whether your family moves or not—but you do have a choice about how you deal with it. Even though leaving your friends and familiar surroundings can be difficult, with effort you can turn it into a positive experience.

As you can see from the *See Jane Win* women quoted on these pages, moving sometimes helped them feel good about themselves and sometimes it caused temporary problems. It was the attitudes of the girls themselves that made the difference. Bragging about your old home and complaining about your new school (like Lisa Hayes-Taylor might have done when she was "hard on everybody") is not likely to make your new classmates love you. After all, the kids at the new school probably like it there. And even if they don't, they don't want to hear it criticized by someone new!

If you make the best of your situation, your new classmates are more likely to accept you. Soon you'll meet kids who share your interests, and then you may really start to feel at home. Until you do, though, here are some tips for dealing with the adjustment:

Host a farewell party for yourself: Before you leave your old home, plan a get-together with your friends. Make sure to get everyone's address, email address,

and phone number. You may also want them to sign an autograph book for you. You can also exchange photographs and tape recordings with kids you're especially close to. When you move, you can keep these reminders of the past in your new room to cheer you up. You can also phone each other or write letters and emails, and maybe even plan visits. You can stay in touch if you want to.

Look for the new place's advantages: Look for maps of the new place in the library and on the Internet. Borrow books about it from the library. Visit it before moving day if you can, and make a list of things that interest you and that you may like about it. Approach the change as you would any other type of travel, with a spirit of discovery. It's a new place with new people to meet, things to do, and sights to see. Think of it as an adventure!

Find out how the school's different: Your parents might have to help you with this one. If you can, get a sense of whether the schoolwork will be easier, harder, or about the same as at your old school. If you think the differences will be small, then your academic adjustments should be easy. If you suspect the new school will be tougher, tell your mom or dad that you may need tutoring. Maybe you and your parent can talk to a guidance counselor or a teacher about this. The new school may even have a peer tutoring program— which is a way to meet new classmates. If the new school looks like it will be less challenging than your old school, ask if your dad or mom can look for enrichment

opportunities in the area, or even a different school. You can also talk to individual teachers about your dilemma. Maybe there are ways they can help you out right in their own classroom.

Be active in trying to make new friends: Even before you get to school, see if you can meet kids in the new neighborhood, and see if they can introduce you to their friends. Many schools pair new kids with a buddy to show them around. This starts you off knowing at least one person on your first day. Some schools have a friendship group to help new students

meet people. It may take a little time before you make real friends, but look for opportunities. For example, if you see a kid you think you might have something in common with, take a risk—walk up to him or her in the hall and say hello.

Observe before you join: It's great to be a joiner, but there's no need to rush into anything at your school. Find out about the clubs and activities. Keep your eyes and ears open to get a sense of who you might like to get to know. Getting in with the wrong crowd can be stressful, so look for friends who share your basic interests and values. Being selective at the beginning can result in better friendships down the road.

Try to be upbeat: Sitting around moping and feeling sorry for yourself is not likely to help you. The more positive you are, the less painful the adjustment is likely to be. So see what you can do to make the best of the situation. Give it your best I CAN girl attitude!

My fascination with international politics began when my family moved to North Africa when I was in second grade. Suddenly we had a full-time maid and traveled to places like Fez and Marrakech.

Then we moved to Arizona when I was twelve. I was thrown into a large and very rough inner-city school. I didn't fit in and was seriously unhappy.

Midway through my freshman year, we moved to southern California. I fell in with a nice group of kids and got involved in speech and debate. My senior year, my dad was transferred to northern California. My parents said if I could find a suitable place to live, I could stay and finish up school rather than move with them. Finally, an English teacher invited me to stay with her family. She made helping me to get into a good college her project. It was an incredible opportunity.

—**Marsha Evans, President, American Red Cross and Retired Rear Admiral, U.S. Navy**

When I was eleven, we left upstate New York and decided to seek our fortune out West. We were traveling to Southern California and had packed everything we owned in a U-Haul. When we got to the Hoover Dam, there were wooden signs inviting us to come to Las Vegas, only 30 miles away. My parents decided to stop in Las Vegas for the night. We never left. The best thing my parents ever did for me was to move to Las Vegas. It opened up opportunities that I couldn't have had anywhere else. It's not so much that I grew up in Las Vegas as I grew up with Las Vegas.

—**Shelley Berkley, U.S. Congresswoman from Nevada**

So, Where Are They Now?

If you're wondering how moving affected the *See Jane Win* women quoted on these pages, here are some answers: Lisa Hayes-Taylor is a teacher in the same Florida schools where teachers once helped her adjust to her move. Shelley Berkley loved Las Vegas so much that she stayed and became a congresswoman. Dr. Susan Lemagie never liked her high school, but it taught her what she did *not* want when she chose a college. It also inspired her to become an educational leader when it came time to help make her own children's schools right for them.

And Marsha Evans, who moved many times because her father was in the Navy, learned to enjoy the adventure of moving. She joined the Navy herself and was eventually promoted to its highest rank, rear admiral—something not many women have managed to achieve. When she retired, she moved to New York City to become first the executive director of the Girl Scouts of the USA and later the president of the American Red Cross.

And the Survey Says:
The parents of fourteen percent of the *See Jane Win* women were divorced while their daughters were growing up.

Going Through a Divorce

Disagreements and arguments are a fact of life, even in a good marriage. So if you hear your parents argue once in a while, that doesn't necessarily mean that their marriage is in trouble. But if a divorce does happen in your family, use these tips to help yourself deal with it:

Don't blame yourself: Kids often worry that they caused their parents' problems. But there's much more to a divorce than kids can ever cause. Your parents probably can't or won't share the details of their problems with you, but be sure not to blame yourself.

It's okay to love both parents. Sometimes it may seem like a divorce is more one parent's fault than the other. One of your parents may even try to get you to see the divorce his or her way. That's natural, because that parent may be mad at your other parent, but it can be confusing to you. Trust your own emotions and don't feel that you have to take sides. You can love both your parents, and you can also be upset or mad at one or both of them.

See a counselor: If you start to feel really sad, and don't know who you can talk to about it, find out how to make an appointment with a school counselor or ask a parent if you can see a private counselor instead. A counselor's job is to help you sort things out—not to take your mom's side or your dad's but just to be there for you. Since counselors can't read minds, you'll need to do your part by talking about your feelings—even when they confuse you. But after a while you'll probably find that talking about your worries helps you cope with them.

Look for other adults you can count on: When parents go through a divorce, kids often feel that their parents are so wrapped up in their own problems that they don't have enough time to hear about what their kids are going through. Remember that there are other adults you can turn to for hugs, counseling, and a sympathetic ear—all the things that you might usually turn to a parent for. Elizabeth Dabrowski, a chemistry teacher, found that after her parents divorced her uncles were always there for her. So in school, when the kids made Father's Day cards, she would cross out the word father, and write uncle instead.

Be patient: If you find out that your parents are getting divorced, you'll probably be left with lots of questions: Who will I live with? Where will we live? Will I have to move or change schools? How often will I get to see the parent who won't live with me? You may feel frightened and worried until your parents work out the custody arrangements. Hopefully, both your parents will help you adjust. And even if they don't both help, you'll settle into a new routine after some time has passed. Some kids even say they like life better after a divorce because they don't hear as many arguments at home.

Stay involved: Keep up with your homework and other activities while your parents' divorce is taking place. Staying active can help you to keep your mind off things that make you sad and that you can't change anyway. You don't need the added stress of falling behind in your schoolwork. And you still can have fun during times that are emotionally hard. Take time to talk and sort out your feelings, but stay involved in things that you're already used to—like school, homework, friendships, and clubs— because they can help you to feel more secure. Since some important arrangements are likely to change in your life, it's good to keep other things in place.

> My parents divorced when I was twelve, and my mother remarried later and had another child. I didn't see my father much because we all lived with my mother, but I knew he was looking out for me because he would call and make sure I was okay, and he wanted to know what was going on. I've always felt my dad was cheering me and my siblings on.
>
> –Pauline Robitaille, Nurse and Director of Surgical Services

If instead of you, it's a friend whose family is going through a divorce, remember that—even though your friend may not always be at her best—she needs you now more than ever. You don't have to side with her mom or dad, only with her. Be a good listener and let her share her feelings. If she seems especially sad, encourage her to talk to a counselor.

One thing I didn't like about my Catholic school was that we were always being told that our parents would go to Hell if they were divorced. No way did I believe my smart, hardworking, divorced mother would ever deserve that! I remember hearing the priest say, "Kids who are troublemakers come from broken homes." I knew the priests were wrong because my mother was so good, and I was trying to be good, too.

–Elizabeth Dabrowski, Chemistry Teacher

My parents divorced when I was about thirteen. All four of us kids shuttled back and forth from Mom's house, which was a little chaotic but fairly normal, to my Dad's house. He had remarried, and was living with his new wife, seven kids, a chimpanzee, and a German shepherd. The divorce was hard on us because my mother was devastated and felt driven to talk about everything to me because that's the way she worked through it. It was hard for me to understand it, but she and I were very close.

–Annik LaFarge, Senior Vice President and E-Publisher, Contentville.com

And the Survey Says: Almost half of all *See Jane Win* women experienced a serious illness or a death in their family by the time they were in middle school.

Facing Health Issues Head-on

If you and your family eat right, get plenty of exercise and rest, and do all the other things that lead to good health, chances are you won't get sick very often. But health problems and accidents still can occur. An occasional sickness, doctors say, can actually help your body fight off

more serious illnesses later. How's *that* for looking at things in the most positive way possible?

But many *See Jane Win* women say that serious health issues have made them stronger. Business executive Tamara Minick-Scokalo was born with a dislocated hip and had to wear a body cast and leg braces for a long time. Some kids not only made fun of her, they pushed her down and then laughed as they watched her struggle to get up. She says this made her become "a champion of underdogs and a protector of the picked on." She stuck up for people who needed help and encouragement, and stood up to people who bullied others the way she was bullied when she was a kid.

There's an expression, "Every cloud has a silver lining." The trick, then, is to try to figure out what the silver lining is. That's what orthopedic surgeon Ruth O'Keefe did when she was in high school, playing in her school band. She was in a bad accident. "I smacked my mouth, injuring my teeth," she says, "so I couldn't really play my horn anymore." It was awful at the time, but that was when she started hanging around the school's chemistry lab and became interested in science—something that she might never have found out about otherwise. "Thank goodness for the accident!" she now says.

Other women have done the same thing. Because Chantel Dothey's mother had multiple sclerosis, Chantel learned early on how to be a caretaker in her family. So did Marsha Evans, whose mother had polio. Today, both have careers that allow them to help others. Chantel is a physician and Marsha is president of the American Red Cross, an organization that helps people cope with diseases, fires, natural disasters, and other emergencies.

You may feel like there's nothing you can do about an illness or an accident in the family, but there are often ways you can help out, even if they're small. You can nurse a sick family relative, help with household chores, or find ways to cheer up or entertain the person who's sick.

Coping with a serious illness can teach you to be strong, patient, sensitive, and helpful. It can also remind you how important taking care of your own health is. Accidents and illnesses are not good, but they can happen to anyone. All an I CAN girl can do is learn from these situations, and try to make the best of things.

> *My mother had multiple sclerosis when I was five. It made me aware at a young age of the reality of life. She would give me a list, and I would get groceries instead of visiting with friends. I had some adult responsibilities, but I was missing something. We were taking care of her instead of the other way around.*
>
> **–Dr. Chantel Dothey, Physician**

> *One of my earliest memories is my mother becoming ill with a mild form of polio while my dad was gone in the Navy. I helped her as much as I could. I can remember leaning over a playpen, changing my baby brother's diaper. The experience of seeing my mother cope made a strong impression about how challenging life was for her.*
>
> **–Marsha Evans, President, American Red Cross, and Retired Rear Admiral, U.S. Navy**

When the Worst Things DON'T Turn Out for the Best

Most people get over, or learn to adjust to, their illnesses. Then they go on with their lives. But sometimes a friend, or a family member, or a pet doesn't get better.

Artist Sandra Sheets* adored her smart, loving father, but he died when she was only eight. Her mother didn't cope well with her husband's death and gambled away all the insurance money. Eventually Sandra had to drop out of high school to support her mother. She loved and cared for her mother, despite her mother's problems. Sandra's sister felt bitter toward their mother. "We look very similar to each other," Sandra says about her sister, "only her mouth is always turned down and mine is more likely to be turned up in a smile." Sandra's optimism and perseverance helped her through some difficult times, and she finally became the artist she hoped to become.

Former *Cosmopolitan* editor-in-chief Helen Gurley Brown's father died in an accident when she was ten. Because of her dad's death, Helen couldn't afford to go on to college, even though she was class valedictorian.

Still, Helen's memories of her dad inspired her. He had always encouraged her to enter writing contests, and she had won one of them. So it's no surprise that she became a writer and an editor. No wonder some people believe that after

someone dies they live on through those who remember them!

Any way you look at it, though, the loss of someone you love isn't easy. So don't be embarrassed if you feel sad and cry sometimes. Wounds like these take a long time to heal. You and the others who are suffering this same loss will need lots of love and support from family members and friends during this painful time. So cut yourself some slack and allow others to pamper you if they want to. Don't be afraid to ask to talk to a counselor who can help you work through the shock, heartache, and pain.

Who Is That Person in My Room?

Susan Widham's house was destroyed in a fire when she was a kid, and she had to go live with her aunt and uncle until her own home could be rebuilt. It was tough to be away from her parents, and her cousin, who was an only child, wasn't happy about sharing her room—and her parents' attention—with Susan.

It's not all that uncommon for kids to have to adjust to living with new people—because a parent remarries or becomes too ill to care for her own children or has an older relative, or a sick one, come to live with the family or adopts a new child or becomes pregnant. Events like these can lead to all kinds of changes in a family routine.

What can an I CAN girl like you do to adjust to changes like these? Here are some ideas that you may wish to try:

Try to understand other people's points of view: Although Susan felt that her cousin didn't welcome her, both kids probably could have shown more empathy for the other one. After all, Susan had just lost her home in a fire, but her cousin's life was interrupted, too. Whether you go to live with others or they come to live with you, it always helps to imagine yourself in the other person's shoes. Your grandmother, for example, might feel like she's in the way because she can't take care of herself alone anymore. Your new stepbrother may still be getting used to not having both his parents around. A foster child may be wondering whether she's wanted anywhere! So try to be patient and to see the change from the other person's point of view. With luck, the other person will try to see things from your point of view as well. That way, everyone involved can enjoy the great rewards of being understanding.

Look for compromises that make life easier for everyone: If things become really difficult with an extra person around, offer suggestions that may make the adjustment easier for everyone. Do you have a basement, attic, or den that, with a little work, could become an extra room? If there are always fights over the bathroom, can you all agree to a schedule for showers and baths? For every problem, there tends to be a solution and an I CAN girl searches for these. She stays flexible and looks for ways to make things work out for everyone.

Keep a journal where you can express your feelings and worries: Writing in a journal can help you vent your frustrations and anger. Talk to the journal as you would talk to a best friend. List some ideas that can help you adjust to the difficulties. Or write about what's going on from someone else's point of view. Challenge yourself to write about positive things that might come out of your situation. That's what people mean when they say, "Take lemons and make lemonade."

Preserve a little private time and space for yourself: Even if you're asked to share your room, you should still make sure that you have some time alone every day. You can take a walk, look for a nook you can hide out in, or put on headphones and tune out the world. If anyone starts to worry about you, explain why you need to withdraw for a while. After an hour or so, you may feel ready to rejoin the group.

Remember that changes are only changes until you get used to them: Sometimes the people joining your family will only stay temporarily. Other times they become an accepted part of your routine and you'd miss them if they were gone. Time helps us adjust to new things. After a while, they aren't new anymore. You may feel like this is the way things have always been! You may even wonder how you ever enjoyed being an only child or not seeing your grandpa at dinner every day.

Speak with someone who can help you to sort things out: If you feel like your mom or dad are too hassled to listen to your worries, look for friends, aunts, grandparents, and other relatives, or a caring school counselor.

Be fair to the other people involved: Even if you're unhappy with a particular change, it makes no sense to make others miserable, too. Acting mean toward your grandma or stepbrother doesn't help. Neither does refusing to notice the new baby. Try to be as welcoming toward others as possible. Draw a picture for your grandma, play a game with your stepbrother, or offer to feed the baby her bottle. In the process of making others happier, your own feelings of peace and well-being may grow.

I CAN!

Tips for How You Can
Deal with Big Changes in Your Life

- Think about changes as a chance to learn something new.

- Keep a positive attitude, even when things seem pretty bad. Chances are they'll get better again soon.

- Reach out for help from someone you trust when you need advice, support, or a shoulder to cry on.

- Even when things change dramatically in your life, hold onto some parts of your routine if you can.

- Take care of your own health as much as you can. The better you feel physically, the easier it will be to cope with whatever else comes along.

- Look for ways to compromise with others and remember that they may be going through as hard a time as you are. Try to see things from their point of view as well as your own.

- Keep a journal and find other ways to enjoy some private time.

- Enjoy change whenever you can. It's an unavoidable part of life.

Chapter 8

My Role Model, My Mentor

Think about how many people you have a chance to observe daily—in your home, at school, in your neighborhood, on TV, in magazines, at the movies, and anywhere else you look. The way they look and act, the things they do, their attitudes can all affect you. Remember back when you were a little kid playing mommy, firefighter, teacher, or movie star. How did you know about these people and what they were like? You had role models all around you to help you form your ideas.

A role model is anyone whose activities or behaviors you learn from and imitate. But a mentor is that—and much more. Mentors are people you know personally—parents, aunts, uncles, grandparents, teachers, Scout leaders, tutors, music or athletic coaches, guidance counselors, religious leaders at your place of worship—anyone who is intentionally trying to help you learn things you need to know. So you could say that mentors are also role models but that role models are not always mentors!

What Do Mentors Do?

The word *mentor* comes from an ancient Greek story, *The Odyssey*, which was written in the eighth century B.C. In the story, a character named Mentor is given the job of educating King Odysseus' son and helping him to become an adult. For some people—like parents, teachers, and athletic coaches—being a mentor and helping you grow into adulthood is part of their job. You don't have to go looking for them. But you can find other mentors. A mentor is any adult that you turn to for help or advice, a sympathetic ear when something's troubling you, tutoring if you're having problems in school, or information about a particular topic or career that interests you. And these are just some of the things mentors can do!

Some grown-ups serve as informal mentors. They're good friends who also happen to be adults. You might work on projects with them, try new things, go on trips to places you might not otherwise get to see. These mentors can also help you set goals, make informed decisions about your life, and give you an outsider's opinion on problems with your family, friends, or school.

Another type of mentorship is more formal. An adult who's an expert in some area agrees to share that knowledge with someone who wants to learn. A plant lover might want a mentor who works at a garden center. Someone who's interested in medicine might want a mentor at a hospital, medical center, or doctor's office. What about you—what would you want your mentor to be like and do?

> *My spiritual passion was nurtured by a variety of role models. My father wasn't intensely involved in religion, but I saw him as a very spiritual man. Other role models included an Orthodox rabbi's wife, a Hebrew school teacher, my mother's Catholic friend who lived with us and went to mass every day, a Lutheran male friend in high school, and finally my grandmother, who died before I was born but who I heard so much about. They were all role models for me. They were all passionate about their religions and I knew I wanted a very spiritual lifestyle.*
>
> **–Miriam Kahane*, Rabbi**

Mentor Wanted: Apply Here!

Mentors can help you look at yourself and your ambitions in new ways. Many of the *See Jane Win* women didn't know what they would have done without these people in their lives! Neurosurgeon Alexa Canady was lucky to count two of the four female neurosurgeons in the

country among her mentors when she was in medical school. Without them, she might never have broken into this male-dominated field. Plant physiologist Camellia Okpodu's mentor taught her to dress for success. "From her I learned that appearances do count," Camellia says. "She was very motivating and had the utmost belief in me."

Interested in finding a mentor of your own? To figure out what type of mentorship you're looking for, ask yourself these questions:

- Why do I want a mentor?
- What do I hope to get from this relationship?
- What type of adult would I get along with best?
- Are there any special skills or interests that I want my mentor to have?
- What can I do to help my mentor bring out the best in me?
- How can I help my mentor in return?

Then make a list of people who might be good mentors to you, or who could point you in the direction of someone who would be. Your mom, dad, or school guidance counselor may be able to suggest people for you to talk to, or provide you with information about mentoring programs that you can apply to. See pages 118–119 for additional resources you can look into as well.

Once you've found someone who might make a good mentor for you, let your mom or dad know that you want to visit, call, write, or email that person. Once you have a parent's okay, go ahead and get in touch. Ask straight-out if she or he is interested in mentoring you. If the person says yes, great! Together the two of you can figure out details of where, when, and how often to meet, what to discuss, and what you can do together. If the person is too busy or has other reasons for saying no, thank her or him and move on. Don't be insulted, and don't worry about it. There are plenty of other great mentors out there!

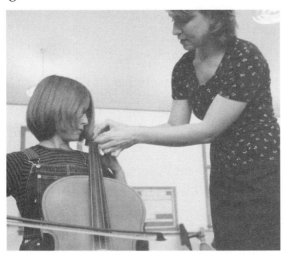

An I CAN Girl Learns About Animals

I just love animals and I was pretty sure I wanted to be a veterinarian. I begged my parents to let me have a dog or a cat. I said, "Mom, I'll take full responsibility for a puppy, and I'll even earn the money for his puppy chow and shots." Mom's answer was definite. "We can't have a pet in our apartment. Our rental agreement doesn't allow it." I knew that my persuading couldn't change a rental agreement.

Then I got this great idea. I went to the animal shelter in our town and asked if I could come once a week to play with pets that needed attention. Mrs. Walter, the woman in charge, said she would give my plan a try. Now I go every Saturday and play with the dogs and cats, but I'm doing much more and learning a lot about caring for pets. I asked Mrs. Walter if she would be my mentor. She's teaching me about animal care and I love learning from her. I feel like I have many pets now and someday I may be in charge of my own animal shelter.—Arielle

A mentorship can last as long as the people involved in it want it to last—a day, a week, a month, a year, or the rest of your life! For a short-term mentorship, you might want to go with a parent or other adult to her or his job one day to find out what goes on in that type of workplace. Or maybe you can visit an adult at work once every week after school for a longer mentorship. If the mentorship really works out, it may grow into a lifelong friendship. That happened to actress, singer, and TV host Florence Henderson. She was so influenced by one of her teachers that they're still in touch.

To make the most of your experience with a mentor, ask questions, take notes, and keep your eyes open. To show your appreciation for the time and knowledge your mentor is offering, be respectful, on time, and on the lookout for useful tasks you could do for your mentor.

> *My mother founded and led two Girl Scout troops of disabled girls at a time when children with disabilities were generally excluded from scouting. Some of the girls in her troops were mentally retarded, some were physically handicapped, and one was blind. My mother loved working with these girls. When she'd observe something that was needed, she'd find a way to meet that need. I watched what she did and applied these same strategies throughout my own career. With her as a role model, I became active in scouting at an early age. Later, I became a teacher who was concerned about educational differences.*
>
> **–Frances Karnes, Ph.D., Professor of Special Education**

And the Survey Says:

Most of the *See Jane Win* women knew and worked with their mentors. But some felt most influenced and guided by deceased relatives who they remembered or heard stories about, or by people they read about in books.

Be a Pick-and-Choose Person

Good role models and mentors are important, but that doesn't mean you become exactly like them or do *everything* their way. As you observe people and hear what they say, or what others say about them, you make choices—consciously or not—about what you take away from each one.

Take Elaine Kraut, for example. Today she is an executive at the mining company her family started when she was a kid. Elaine's mother and aunt helped Elaine's father build the business from the ground up. Her father, she says, was a dreamer with bold ideas, but her mother was practical. She made sure that the ideas they actually pursued were the best ones. Then there was her grandmother, a strong, tall, proud woman. "When Grandma was anywhere around, there was no question about who was in charge of our family," Elaine says.

To this day, Elaine realizes that—although she is not exactly like any of them—she learned something special from each of these important people in her life.

Elaine sees herself as a strong woman with bold, original ideas. Yet she also prides herself on being practical about how to use them. Although Elaine saw her father as her most important role model, all her family members influenced her.

Role models can help you identify the traits you admire, but even people you look up to exhibit some qualities you'd rather not have. After all, everyone has bad days and unpleasant habits. Maybe your dad is normally calm but you sometimes see him get very tense. And maybe your older sister is the nicest person you know, except when her friends come over. Then she becomes so bossy that you'd rather not be around her! You can still learn things from these people. The trick is to take the best from each person.

Since role models and mentors can have a big impact on your life, it's a good idea to be aware of what their actions are teaching you. One way to do that is to look at, and really study, how others deal with the things that matter to you.

For example, if you have a quick temper, make it a point to notice how other people deal with their anger. Some people make a joke of it while others hold it in or lash out. Still others come right out and say what's bothering them. Which responses do you think work best and why? Once you have some answers, you can use what you've learned the next time a tense situation occurs.

Role models can even teach you how to handle situations that you have yet to experience. Next time you watch an awards ceremony on TV, notice how many winners thank a whole list of people who helped them. Pretty impressive, isn't it? Also notice that when the camera focuses on runners-up in the audience, they are usually smiling and applauding the winner. But what about the runner-up who the camera catches sulking, or who makes a nasty comment to the press later, showing what a sore loser she or he is? Or what about the winner who gives an entirely me-centered acceptance speech? What kind of winner or loser would you want to be?

The messages you learn from role models and mentors aren't always clearly defined. The heroes in movies and on TV shows don't give formal lessons on how to do the right thing. Talk-show hosts don't explain how to come up with questions that will get people to speak their mind. But by watching them, you begin to figure these things out for yourself. You pick up messages about people from just about everything they do—from the way they dress to their hairstyles to their table manners to the way they treat others. As you go through life, you'll have to decide for yourself which traits you want to have and which you want to avoid. All of these decisions, put together, help you to become the kind of you that you are!

> *When I used to help my dad on political campaigns, there was a woman at the courthouse who was always nice to me. She looked like the kind of person I'd like to be someday. There was also a woman on the bus I took to school every morning who always seemed angry at her children. I knew I didn't want to grow up to be like her. My sister and cousins were negative about everything, so I didn't want to be like them either. But my most important hero was President Kennedy. His picture still hangs in my courtroom office. He is a role model for my idealism and my wish to make a positive difference in the world.*
>
> **–Edna Conway*, Judge**

The Medium Is the Message

It's hard to believe how strong an impact the images from movies, magazines, and television have on us, but scientific studies tell us that they do. One study shows that kids who watch more than one hour of television a day tend to be more violent than kids who watch less. Kids who view R-rated movies are more likely to become smokers because R-rated movies show more people with cigarettes than G- or PG-rated films do.

TV, movies, and magazines are filled with messages insisting that the happiest, healthiest, and most popular women are thin and beautiful—or at least what's generally considered beautiful at the moment.

You may already realize that this isn't true. Looking like a model, rock star, or actress will not make you happy, but many girls want so desperately to look like the images they see that they develop eating disorders. That doesn't sound like the glamorous lifestyle that magazine ads and TV programs portray!

Fortunately, you can also find positive role models on TV or in movies and magazines. For example, *The Mary Tyler Moore Show,* a situation comedy about a female producer on a television news program, inspired TV's Jane Pauley when she was a teen. Janice Huff, on the other hand, searched in vain for a black female meteorologist on her TV screen. When she couldn't find one, she made up her mind to fill that role herself when she grew up.

Books are another place to look for positive role models. Biographies—books that tell a real person's life story—are a good place to start. Camellia Okpodu, a plant physiologist and African-American, drew courage from reading Booker T. Washington's autobiography, *Up from Slavery*—especially when she felt that she was being discriminated against in school. "I started thinking, if this man had to walk such a distance to get an education and had to be so courageous to learn to read, why do I have the right to sit here and complain because a few people don't think I should be here?" she says.

New Jersey Assemblywoman Mary Previte, who lost her left hand in an accident at fourteen, was particularly inspired when she read about President Franklin Roosevelt, who was paralyzed by polio. He didn't have the strength to lift his own body out of a wheelchair!

The characters in fiction can also have a positive influence on you. Author Jacquelyn Mitchard saw Jo, in Louisa May Alcott's classic novel *Little Women,* as the "writer girl" she wanted to be when she was growing up. Many former I CAN girls, including Wilma P. Mankiller, the first female chief of the Cherokee Nation, were big fans of Nancy Drew books, a series about a girl detective.

Evaluating the Message

It's tough to ignore messages that we see and hear in the media, since we're bombarded by them all the time. But you can learn to be critical about them. When you're looking at TV, magazines, and movies, keep these things in mind:

Your values: Think about what the people on your TV or movie screen do. Should you be impressed with them as human beings, not just for the clothes they wear or the songs that they sing? Which actors and actresses, in their real lives are working for good causes and charities or have values that are in line with yours?

Good health: Your favorite models and rock stars may look really hip, but being too thin is no healthier than eating nothing but the junk food advertised on Saturday morning TV. There's no alternative to healthy food choices and plenty of exercise. So don't spend too much time watching the screen. Get out there and have your own action-packed, exercise-filled adventures instead!

It's nothing like real life: Things don't happen in real life the way they do in movies and on TV. People don't hear music playing in the background when they're falling in love. They don't make up with one another or solve problems within a half hour (not counting commercials). So don't assume you can learn social skills, manners, or the best ways to behave from movies and TV. Producers are more interested in keeping your interest than they are in showing how people truly are.

Imagine a Future You!

Want to take a closer look at how your role models influence you? Here's a way to get started:

1. Make a list of people in your life who matter to you. Begin with family members, then people at school or in other groups or classes you've joined, and finally the role models you find in books and movies and on TV.

2. Next to each person on your list, write the characteristics you most like about her or him. These might include the person's career choice, clothes, way of treating other people, personality—anything.

3. Imagine yourself as an adult with many of these same traits. What might you be doing? How might the qualities you've seen in your role models influence you? Write a paper describing what you imagine. If you like, draw a picture to go with it. (See Alyssa's sample on page 98.)

If you want, show your work to a parent, friend, or teacher, or to some other person you trust. Your teacher might even give you extra credit for it! Save a copy to look at again when you're older. It'll be fun to see whether you grow in the direction of your current dreams or whether your dreams change.

Here's Alyssa's dream description:

Role Models	Characteristics I Admire
MOTHER	STRONG, SMART, UPBEAT, BALANCED
FATHER	ADVENTUROUS, KIND, FUNNY, HARD WORKER
AUNT JANET (PHOTOGRAPHER)	HAS A CAREER AND FAMILY, KEEPS CALM WHEN OTHERS SEEM CRAZED
MR. DILLAHUNT (FOURTH-GRADE TEACHER)	HAPPY, ENERGETIC, KNOWS ALL KINDS OF UNUSUAL THINGS
MRS. KAPOV (GYMNASTICS COACH)	SELF-DISCIPLINED, GOAL DIRECTED, ATHLETIC
MRS. STONE (GIRL SCOUT LEADER)	CREATIVE, STRONG LEADER, WELL ORGANIZED, JUGGLES MANY TASKS AT ONE TIME
HARRIET THE SPY (CHARACTER IN BOOK)	SMART, INDEPENDENT, ADVENTUROUS, GOOD WRITER
KATIE COURIC AND ANN CURRY (NEWS ANCHORS)	HAVE COOL JOBS, GET TO TRAVEL A LOT
VENUS AND SERENA WILLIAMS (TENNIS PLAYERS)	SISTERS, ARE CLOSE WITH EACH OTHER, ALWAYS TRY THEIR BEST, ARE GOOD SPORTS—AND GOOD AT SPORTS

Alyssa's Dreams for the Future

SOMEDAY I'D LIKE TO HAVE A CAREER AND FAMILY LIKE MY AUNT JANET. I HOPE THAT IT'S AN ADVENTUROUS CAREER IN WHICH I'LL GET TO TRAVEL A LOT. MAYBE I COULD BE A PHOTOGRAPHER LIKE SHE IS, OR A TV REPORTER LIKE KATIE COURIC AND ANN CURRY. THEY GET TO SEE AMAZING PARTS OF THE WORLD AND HAVE COOL ADVENTURES. THE BAD THING ABOUT THEIR JOBS IS THAT THEY HAVE TO GET UP SO EARLY IN THE MORNING.

I GUESS WHEN I FIGURE OUT JUST WHAT I WANT TO DO, THE SELF-DISCIPLINE I'M LEARNING FROM MRS. KAPOV, MY GYMNASTICS COACH, WILL COME IN HANDY. SHE'S TAUGHT ME THAT YOU CAN GET MUCH BETTER AT SOMETHING IF YOU KEEP TRYING REALLY HARD. WHATEVER I DO, I HOPE I ALWAYS KEEP LEARNING ALL KINDS OF FUNNY INTERESTING INFORMATION LIKE MY TEACHER MR. DILLAHUNT SHARES WITH US. HE LAUGHS A LOT AND TELLS US FUN FACTS AND STORIES ABOUT THE WORLD THAT I NEVER WOULD HAVE GUESSED.

My mom was a single mom and I don't remember my dad at all, but I had lots of loving parenting from my two uncles, who lived downstairs from us. They were both college graduates, which was pretty unusual in our neighborhood. It was unusual for the time, but my chemist uncle worked in a laboratory with almost all women. They were always willing to take time to answer my questions or explain what they were working on. My other uncle was an attorney and worked for a woman bank president. I didn't even realize that women scientists and bank presidents were the exception.

—Elizabeth Dabrowski, Chemistry Teacher

I CAN!

Tips for How You Can
Get the Most from Role Models and Mentors

THESE MODELS NEED TO EAT A SANDWICH.

- Look for role models that reflect the I CAN girl you want to be. Identify the qualities in others that you'd like to have and focus on learning from those.

- As you observe peoples' actions and behaviors, ask yourself: What do these things really say about them?

- Study the way other people deal with issues that are like ones you deal with. Figure out what you do and don't respect about how they handle them.

- Question what you see and hear on TV and in movies, books, music, and magazines. Ask yourself which messages are honest and which are just meant to sell something. Ignore the selling messages as much as you can.

- Look for mentors who can add value to your life. You can find them either through formal mentoring programs or on your own.

- Remember that people also learn about you through your actions, so try to make choices that will lead others to look up to you!

Chapter 9

All in the Family

> *I had a wonderful mom. I have never been able to figure out how she did it, but my mom brought me up to think that I could be anybody I wanted to be.*
>
> **–Cady Coleman, NASA Astronaut**

> *My father taught me how to play chess. He didn't just let me win, but very early on made it clear that it was unacceptable to throw a tantrum and walk away if I was losing. He would try to reinforce in me that a mistake was only a mistake if I didn't learn from it. I learned to put things in perspective and to tell myself "I'm still doing well; I shouldn't throw in the towel; I can work this out and do better. It's okay not to be the first in everything."*
>
> **–Tamara Minick-Scokalo, Marketing Director, Procter & Gamble**

Take a moment to compare your family with other families you know. Isn't it amazing how much difference you find? Families live in different ways and places. They're big or small and do different kinds of things together. They're even related to each other in different ways. Congresswoman Barbara Cubin, for example, grew up with her mother, three siblings, her stepfather, and his three children. A single mother raised Elizabeth Dabrowski, with help from Elizabeth's uncles. Janice Huff was raised by her single mother and her grandmother and grandfather. And Tamara Minick-Scokalo was the youngest of four sisters in a traditional two-parent family.

Yet all four *See Jane Win* women say they always had plenty of love, respect, and learning in their homes.

> *Although my mom never had the opportunity to play in a major orchestra, she was a fine violinist and still is a good teacher. Perhaps because she was single during so much during my childhood, I saw early on that women need to be able to support themselves.*
>
> **–Louise Behrens*, Orchestral Musician**

> *My mother encouraged me to either walk past obstacles or to push through them, and to this day I call her for advice.*
>
> **–Jeanette Ives Erickson, Senior Vice President, Patient Care Services and Chief of Nursing**

> *I'm the middle child of eleven children. Even compared to other children in our community, we were very poor. We had no television, no indoor plumbing, no electricity, and very little contact with the world outside our community, but we did all kinds of things as a family. My parents had an enormous influence on me. Our home was a gathering place for people in our community.*
>
> **–Wilma P. Mankiller, former Principal Chief, Cherokee Nation**

Lessons Learned at Home

You are constantly learning from your family, and they are learning from you. Whenever family members play games, read or talk together, share a hobby, work side by side, or do anything else together, they're sharing skills, values, and attitudes. Some of these are taught directly. That's what happens if your dad shows you how to compare prices in the supermarket. It's what happens if your mom taught you how to ride a bicycle when you were younger. But you learn other things by watching what family members

do, and how they treat one another. You notice the way your dad takes care of you when you're sick, or the tone of voice your mom uses when she reminds you to help with household chores.

These words, used by the *See Jane Win* women, describe some of the values and attitudes that went along with the other life skills they were taught at home:

Courtesy
Respect
Ambition
Competitiveness
Cooperation
Courage
Thriftiness
Confidence
Neatness
Self-discipline
Independence
Optimism
Humor
Responsibility
Generosity
Sensitivity

How many of these values and attitudes are also important in your family? Which family members have played a big part in teaching them to you? What about those other life skills—like tying your shoelaces, making your bed, washing the dishes, or taking phone messages? Who in your family helped you learn these things . . . and what have you taught them in return?

To think this through in more detail, make a Family Learning Chart:

Chantal's Family Learning Chart

Family Member	What I Have Learned/Can Learn	What I Have Taught/Can Teach
MOM	KINDNESS, CREATIVE WRITING, IMAGINATION	TYPING SKILLS, HOW TO USE THE INTERNET
DAD	BUSINESS, COOKING, BASKETBALL	NEATNESS, NEW DANCE STEPS, AND OTHER POINT OF VIEW
GRANDPA JOE	SPANISH, COOKING	COMPUTER GAMES, BETTER HANDWRITING
GRANDMA	QUILTING, CAT'S CRADLE	TIE-DYING, EMAIL, HOW TO BLOW BUBBLES WITH BUBBLE GUM
NANA	FISHING, SKIPPING STONES	HOW TO USE CHOPSTICKS, HOW TO DO TRICKS WITH A YO-YO.
AUNT ALLISON	ANTIQUES AND ART	NOT SURE
UNCLE ERIC	JOKES, LEADERSHIP, WOODWORKING	CHESS, CARD GAMES, HOW TO SLOW DOWN
UNCLE ALAN	YOGA, HOW TO GROW TOMATOES	MAGIC TRICKS, IN-LINE SKATING
COUSIN DAN	WATER SKIING, PIG LATIN, HOW TO FIX THINGS	COMPROMISING, PATIENCE, DOUBLE DUTCH
COUSIN DAVIDA	MATH, SENSE OF HUMOR, CHEERFULNESS, GYMNASTIC TRICKS	DANCE STEPS, KNITTING, MY FAVORITE GAMES
COUSIN BEN	BRAILLE, HOW TO DO CARTWHEELS	JOKES, CAT'S CRADLE
COUSIN AVI (AGE 2)	BABY-SITTING SKILLS, KINDNESS, HOW TO TALK WITH FEW WORDS	COLORS, NUMBERS, LETTERS, NEW WORDS, SHARING

To make your own Family Learning Chart:

1. Make a copy of the chart on page 103. In the left-hand column, list the family members who play a big part in your life. Don't limit yourself to the people you live with. Include aunts, uncles, cousins, grandparents, and others who are important to you.

2. In the second column, list one (or more) skill, value, or attitude you've learned—or can learn—from each of them. (Look back at Chantal's chart for ideas.)

3. In the third column, list anything that you have taught, or can imagine teaching, each of these people. Really think about this. You'll be amazed how much you have to offer. You may have knowledge and skills—in math, for example, or in computer keyboarding, baton twirling, in-line skating, or ear wiggling. But you may also be well organized, open minded, polite, or patient, and people in your family might find those traits useful themselves. You can also look back at the chart listing your strengths that you created from the chart on page 14. It may give you additional ideas of things you have to teach as well.

My Family Learning Chart

Family Member	What I Have Learned/ Can Learn	What I Have Taught/ Can Teach

Once your chart is completed, take a look at how much you and your family know! If you'd like, use the information on your chart, and anything else you can think of, as the basis for a poem, story, or essay about what you've learned from a particular relative on your list. You may even want to present that person with a copy of it on his or her birthday (or, if it's a parent, on Mother's or Father's Day). This can be a great way to show how much that person means to you!

> *My dad inspired me. He was a carpenter, storyteller, inventor of characters, and very creative thinker. He was also my first art teacher. He and I would sit at the kitchen table and draw and doodle. My father's influence propelled me into the children's book arena because I enjoy the storytelling and fantasy.*
>
> **–Mary GrandPré, Illustrator of the Harry Potter Books**

> *With three younger brothers, I had plenty of nurturing leadership experience. This has helped me as a rabbi, since I often find myself mediating relationships just as I did with my brothers.*
>
> **–Miriam Kahane*, Rabbi**

> *My father used to say, "We don't have much monetarily, but we can have good character and a great reputation. People can take your money, they can take your material possessions, but they can't take your character, and they can't take your reputation. You give that away." We would roll our eyes and say, "Oh, here we go again," but we heard and learned his important messages.*
>
> **–Florence Henderson, Singer, Television Host, and Actor who played the mother on THE BRADY BUNCH**

The Best Way to Give–and Get–an Education at Home

Now that you know how much knowledge you have, why not share some of it with people you are close to? As elementary school teacher Nancy Collier* and environmental engineer Teresa Culver both learned, it's a good feeling to help someone else to learn something new. By helping her brother with his schoolwork, Nancy discovered her interest in teaching. And Teresa stood a little taller whenever her older brother introduced her to his friends as "the smart one."

"It never seemed to bother him to have me help him with his spelling," Teresa remembers. "We spent a lot of time together, he learning and I teaching, and both of us having fun. He seemed so proud that I was a 'brain.'"

If your goal is to teach your cousin how to compromise or your kid sister to be more patient, the best way to go about it is by setting an example. If you want to teach someone a new skill, however—like how to juggle, play chess, or play the kazoo—the lessons will probably be more formal. So first make sure that the person is interested. Listen for them to say something like, "That's so cool, the way you taught yourself those card tricks," or "I wish I could skate as well as you." Then you can also ask straight out if your relative would like you to teach something you know how to do.

Next, find a time that's good for you both. Before the lesson begins, think about the things that help you learn best. Teresa Culver, for example, was motivated by her siblings' encouragement. Kindness, patience, and a sense of humor come in handy when you're coaching, tutoring, or teaching.

Some skills need to be broken down into steps and presented in order. For example, if you want to teach someone how to follow a recipe for brownies, the first thing to do is gather all the ingredients, plus measuring cups, measuring spoons, a mixing bowl, and a pan to bake them in. And you haven't even started measuring yet. Thinking this way makes you realize how many steps are involved even in simple things.

Many people learn best by doing—and even by making mistakes along the way. Maybe your brother's first batch of brownies will burn, or your cousin will wind up with scrapes and bruises the first

time she skates. Your little sister may put her shirt on inside out or button it up the wrong way, and your niece's first braids

may leave her with a head full of crooked-looking knots. It's okay to laugh *with* people you teach, but not at them. Remember how awkward it feels to try something new. But with time and plenty of practice, practice, practice, the learner will be a pro!

What if you're the one trying to learn something new? The process is pretty much the same. But if the teacher gets impatient or starts putting you down, that's a problem. Don't take the risk of losing your confidence because someone's teaching style doesn't match the way you learn best. Stop the lesson, thank the person politely, and explain that you don't feel this is working. If it's a school subject or another skill that's important to learn, have an adult help you look for a different teacher or find another way to learn.

You're sure to feel great when you master a new skill or see a relative or friend master one because of you. And you'll wind up with someone new to share your interest with you!

And the Survey Says:

Most of the *See Jane Win* women women viewed their relationships with their parents positively while they were growing up. Relationships were a little bumpier during adolescence, but most of the women were not very rebellious as teens.

Let's Show Some Respect!

Do you ever laugh at the way kids on TV disrespect people? Maybe you saw a sit-com where kids made fun of a mom who accidentally wallpapered a door shut, or a guy who locked himself in a basement. Or maybe it was a program where kids out-smarted an adult in some way. It's fun to laugh and joke around *with* family and friends, but no one appreciates being laughed *at* the way we laugh at characters on TV—or the way they sometimes laugh at each other.

How can you show respect to family members and others? One way is by listening, by really taking in what they tell you, and by never poking fun at the things that they do. You can also show respect by staying calm and keeping your voice down, even when you really, *really* disagree with a person. No matter who that person is, you can win more respect by showing how mature and disciplined you are than by yelling. You'll find that people are more likely to consider your viewpoint and be respectful of you when you're respectful yourself.

I come from a very close family that values honesty and working hard for what we have. We were taught to be frugal. I never felt I had to do without, but we were always careful with money. We were expected to do well in school and go to college. Community service was another important part of my parents' lives that has influenced my life, and now, hopefully, I am passing that on to my children.

–Jan Dorman, Homemaker, Community Leader

My mother wrote a neighborhood news column and was a court reporter. She used to teach us a word a day. My dad engaged me in outdoor adventures, and I appreciated learning that from him. Our family sat around the kitchen table at dinnertime and talked about news events, politics, the world, and how leaders in the world effected change. I thought about how I could effect change in some way.

–Kathleen Dunn, Public Radio Host

> *Although she only had a fifth-grade education, my grandmother taught me to read and spell using the Bible when I was four. She taught me the Proverbs and to love poetry. She said, "A good name will go farther than you will ever go." The words of my grandmother come back to me even now. I have a deep family pride.*
>
> **–Marva Collins, Founder, Marva Collins Preparatory School, Chicago**

> *My siblings and I never had any huge gripes with our parents in middle or high school. There simply was no major rebellion. We were all very goal directed and independent. However, that doesn't mean we didn't go through a stage when we thought we knew more than our parents.*
>
> **–Dr. Alice Petrulis, Physician**

Of course, family feuds and disagreements do happen. People get on each other's nerves at least once in a while. They say things they don't mean, they blame others when things go wrong, and they argue over things they have to share or over whose turn it is to set the table or wash the dishes.

We all have moods. You can't change other people's personalities. But you can change how you treat them and how you handle disagreements. Being considerate goes a long way toward smoothing out a conflict—even before it starts, sometimes. For example, if you play your music quietly, no one has to ask you to turn it down. Offer to compromise or take turns choosing what TV shows to watch. You might even let your sister borrow your favorite sweater because she's going to a party. If you do, she's more likely to do you a favor in return.

As a kid, public relations director Mabel Barry* was grounded whenever she didn't keep the curfew that her parents gave her. But when she finally learned to respect their rules, her parents started to offer her more liberties and respect her ability to make good decisions.

Community leader Jan Dorman found that being respectful had other benefits also. When she was eight, her dad was appointed to the House of Delegates in Maryland. Jan and her siblings had to learn to shake hands, go to parades, and listen attentively whenever her father gave public speeches. "By nature, I was introverted," Jan says. "But since it was expected of me, I stepped outside myself and performed those activities, and it built my social confidence."

In general, kids are most likely to be disrespectful when they're sad, frustrated, or angry—or when they're imitating real or TV-show kids who have negative attitudes. So keep an eye on your own behavior. Don't let things get to the point where people have to tell you to stop sassing them. Show that you have the self-discipline to control your behavior on your own.

What to Do When You're Angry, Frustrated, or Sad

Getting older doesn't give you the right to talk disrespectfully. You're more likely to be heard if you can stay calm. If your goal is to win respect, start by giving it to others. Before you lose your temper, try to do these things instead:

Take Time Out: Go to your room or take a walk. Some people will take a nap. They find that getting some rest helps them feel more rational. If you can't find a chance to be alone right away, take a deep breath and slowly count to ten before you say anything you might regret later on.

Explain Your Feelings: You can say, "Mom, I feel too angry to talk about this right now. I just need time to feel mad (or sad) and then to calm down." Then, once you feel ready, ask to discuss whatever it was that upset you. When you make the first move, you show that you're willing to deal with serious issues head-on.

Punch a mattress or pillow: Sometimes you just have to get out the anger that's in you. When this happens, find a punching bag, or make one. Just be sure it's something that won't break and won't make a lot of noise.

Write a letter or journal entry: Writing about how you feel can put things in perspective and may help release some of your anger. You can also write to a friend. Or you can write the person you're mad at, beginning with the words, "Here's a note telling you how I feel." Once you're calmer, you can decide whether to send the note or tear it up.

Hug Your Pet: Pets have a calming effect on most people. It's almost as if they sense your frustrations. You can pour your feelings out to them the way you do in a diary. They don't talk back, and with a purr or a lick they can help you smile again.

When You and a Parent Disagree

Even when you disagree with a parent—let's say it's your dad—you probably know that he's trying to do what's in everyone's best interest. That's especially true when it comes to topics like staying out late, eating dessert when you haven't eaten dinner, or buying things you don't really need. In cases like these, why argue? You can say, "I'm disappointed," or even, "I'm angry," but you may as well accept—and respect—his decision. After all, if you're clear on the reasons behind it, then you understand why he made it. If the reasons aren't clear to you, then ask what they are—politely. Or if you understand but don't agree, you might (calmly) say, "Okay, I understand and I'll do what you tell me. But please, I would appreciate it if you could hear me out and consider my point of view before you make up your mind and say yes or no."

If you're given a chance to state your case, say what you have to say and then wait patiently. You're more likely to get a yes if you do. No matter how the decision goes, though, don't be pushy. Allow your dad to think before answering. If your argument's convincing, you may just get your way.

And it doesn't matter whether your parents live together or apart—don't play them against each other. If you're pretty sure your dad's going to give you an answer you don't want to hear, don't avoid it by going to your mom first to get her okay. Not only is that disrespectful, but if your parents figure out what you're doing, they'll both be mad at you!

If your dad's final verdict is a no, then that's it: Let it go. You won't get anywhere by arguing. You may even make him less willing to listen the next time.

How to Talk So a Parent Will Listen

What do you do if you . . .

- are being bullied at school?
- had a big fight with your best friend?
- heard a story on the news that left you with nightmares?
- overheard a conversation about you that bothers you?
- feel upset about something?

It's great to feel that you can confide in a parent, but sometimes and for some people, that isn't easy. You may be afraid that your mom won't listen, your dad won't understand, your foster mother will worry too much, or your grandfather will get angry.

"Nah, it's not worth it," you decide. Then you head off to talk to your friend, brother, sister, hamster, turtle, parakeet, dog, or cat, about whatever's troubling you.

But even if your friend, brother, or pet is the best listener in the world, don't give up on trying to talk with your parent! Being able to talk with the adults in your home will leave you better able to talk with others throughout your life. Besides, they may have some good suggestions for you. After all, they were kids once, and probably remember what it was like to be bullied, frightened, or left out of a group. Hearing about what happened to them could give you a new way of seeing your

problems, and they may be able to suggest new ways of dealing with the problem.

With that in mind, here are some ways to make it easier to talk with a parent:

Find the right time to talk: You probably already know not to start a conversation with your stepmom when she's on the phone, paying bills, or cleaning up the glass of juice your little sister just spilled. Better times include: right before bed or when the two of you are hanging out at home together or on your way somewhere. If she always seems too busy, ask for an appointment. Make it clear that you have something on your mind and need to talk. You might even try to schedule a daily or weekly parent (or family) talk time, so you won't have to wait for a crisis.

Practice what you want to say: You might even write a list so you won't forget anything important. This will help make it clear that the problem is serious and that you've already put some thought into it. It may make your parent listen more closely and spend more time looking for solutions.

Work up the courage to speak out: When it comes to talking about tough stuff with a parent, it's harder for some kids to find courage than time! If this is true for you, ask yourself why that is. Are you afraid of disagreements, or that your parent won't understand or won't listen or won't care what you say? Once you've pinpointed your fears, start your conversation by getting them out in the open. You might say, "I want to ask you something, but I'm afraid that you'll be mad," or "I have something to tell you, but I'm afraid you'll interrupt me before I get it all out." This way the grown-up can respond to them right from the start. They may even say something like, "I'll try not to be angry," or "I'll do what I can to listen until you are done." Of course, it still may not happen, but it may at least get the grown-ups to stop, think, and try to understand how you feel.

Be prepared to listen and consider what you hear: Let's say you're talking to your foster mother. If you want her to keep an open mind with you, you'll need to keep one as well. That means really listening to what she says. You might even take notes while she's speaking. Then you can go back and think about what she told you. If you cut her off instead, saying things like, "I know that," you may miss a really good suggestion that was coming after the one you'd already thought of.

If all else fails, find another adult you trust: Sometimes a grandparent, an aunt, an uncle, a teacher, a religious or scout leader, a school counselor, or a good friend's parent can help you through your struggles when your own parent can't. Or one of those people may be able to suggest someone else who can. You never have to be alone with your problems. Look around for a trustworthy adult. But the word *trust* here is important. Don't tell your problems to strangers, including people on the Internet—even if they seem fine, and are trying to convince you that they have your best interests at heart.

Following in a Brother's or Sister's Footsteps . . . or Not

When she was growing up, Martha Aarons always dreaded the first day of math class. "I'd walk in, and the teacher would say, 'Are you Charlie Aarons's sister? He was such a great student! I hope you'll be just as smart.'"

All through school Martha avoided math and the harder sciences as much as she could. She steered clear of subjects that would throw her into head-on competition with her brother. Luckily for her, though, Martha was good in some subjects that her brother wasn't. No wonder she wound up in a music-related career!

Even so, Martha did well on the math section of the SATs, a test many kids take if they're applying to college. It showed her that she was better at math than she had thought. She realized she could have done better in her math classes if she had given them a chance.

You don't have to be good at the same things as the other kids in your family—but don't immediately reject these subjects without giving them a fair try. Rather than think, "I'll seem dumb if I'm not as good as my brother," tell yourself, "My brother is really good at this subject, so maybe a talent runs in our family. I may be good at it too." Why not? You never know!

It's also fine to get interested in something the other kids in your family aren't good at. You don't have to be the same as anyone, or different from anyone. Just be an I CAN girl and look for your own interests and strengths.

> *My mother and sister were smashingly beautiful, and my brother and father were very handsome. I thought my plain appearance set me apart from the family, but as I look back I realize I was just normal looking. My mother would say, "Becky has the looks and Anne has the brains." I interpreted that as, "You're bright but not very attractive, and so you'd better develop your intelligence." I think my sister was most disadvantaged by the comparison. She was just as bright as I was. She was very creative and an excellent writer as a child, but my family never considered her to be smart. As a result, my sister underachieved and never attended college.*
>
> —Anne Caroles*, Ph.D., Psychologist

> *I was number two of five children, behind an older sister who as a child was accident prone and sickly with rheumatic fever. My mother delegated some of her care to me, so I played nurse to my older sister. Maybe that's where I learned my caretaker role. Following me are two brothers and a sister. We looked out for each other and remain very close.*
>
> **–Jeanette Ives Erickson, Senior Vice President, Patient Care Services and Chief of Nursing**

On the Business of Birth Order

According to many experts, your placement in a family—whether you're the oldest, the youngest, or somewhere in the middle—can have a big effect on you. So can the number of girls and boys in your household. Oldest children tend to be most comfortable taking on leadership positions. (So if you're the oldest child, let the younger kids take charge once in a while.) The youngest kids are generally more social and creative. (If this is you, make sure you take some time to be by yourself.) Middle kids often feel left out. (If you're a middle kid, focus on your interests and accomplishments and let your parents know when you need time and attention from them.) Only children are often independent and feel comfortable spending time alone. (If you're an only child, don't isolate yourself. Get to know your cousins and other relatives if you can, and don't be shy about making friends.)

In a family of all girls, one is likely to take an interest in activities that some people associate with boys. If that's you, you may be more comfortable than your sisters with adventure, competition, getting dirty, and fixing things. On the other hand, if you're a girl surrounded by brothers, you may need to fight for the opportunity to take on a leadership role. You'll have to learn to say, "Now it's my turn to light the campfire, Isaac," or "Come on, David—set the table. I did it yesterday."

So be sure to assert your rights as an I CAN girl—even when your brother is an I CAN boy!

> *I was one of five children—all girls. Because my dad had no sons, he did things with me he probably would not have otherwise. He would often have me help him fix an engine, repack wheel bearings, and help him with house repairs. Because of him, I was motivated to take shop and electrical classes in high school.*
>
> **–Angela Sands*, Registered Nurse**

An I CAN Girl Learns to Be All She Can Be

My name is Rachel and I'm a middle sister. My oldest sister, Carrie, is really smart and is in honors everything. Then there's my baby brother, Sam. He's not even in kindergarten yet but he can read, add, and subtract. I keep hearing how smart he is, too.

So when the teacher said I didn't make it into honors math I figured maybe I just wasn't as smart as Carrie and Sam. Then that same teacher showed my parents my math test scores, which were really high, and they got all upset. My mom said to the teacher, "If she can get such high test scores, why aren't you putting her in honors math?" The teacher told her that I was probably just lucky on that one test. I agreed because I felt really dumb in math class.

Mom pushed a little and finally the teacher said she'd give me a trial period in honors math. I didn't really want a trial period. I was sure honors math would be too hard and I just gave up. Sometimes I didn't even hand in my work. I'd get Fs. Then I'd get Bs and Cs on tests and that wasn't too bad until my mom had this idea I was an underachiever. I didn't think that was my problem. I figured that those high test scores had fooled my parents and that I could never do as well as they thought I should.

Anyway, my mom took me to see this psychologist, Dr. Sylvia Rimm, who specializes in smart kids who are having problems in school. She tested me again and I was surprised when she agreed with my parents. She said her tests showed that I had especially good spatial skills, which meant that I'd probably get even better at math as it got harder. I started to think that if they all believe I'm that smart, maybe they're right. So I decided I'd try a little harder.

It's funny, but as soon as I did, my grades went up a little. Soon I started getting 90s and 100s on quizzes and I even got a 95 on a big test. Wow— I never thought I could be that smart. I thought my sister and brother had the brains and I was just the more friendly and social one. I'm starting to feel different now. I think maybe I'm really pretty smart, too, and that those test grades weren't just lucky. Maybe when you work at something you make your own luck. Now I just hope my sister and brother don't mind having another smart kid in the family.

I CAN!

Tips for How You Can
Learn and Grow with Your Family

- Think about how much you and your family can learn from each other. Then think up ways you can foster that learning.

- Be patient and encouraging when helping others—and ask people to be patient and encouraging with you.

- Show respect to everyone in your family.

- Use your actions and tone of voice to show family members how mature you can be. It will help you gain their respect and your independence.

- When you have something important to say to a family member, find a time, place, and way to say it that will help you make sure that you're heard.

- You don't have to follow the same paths in life as your brothers, sisters, or other family members, but you don't have to avoid them either. Just pick those that seem right for you.

And Lastly...

Go for the Goal!

Many people (including psychologists) used to believe that all women should do in life was get married and have children. They believed that women didn't need careers outside the home or beliefs of their own. But that was then. This is now. Today, girls are expected to set goals for themselves and move out into the world. They're expected to decide for themselves who they want to be and what they want to do. This is a wonderful thing—but it isn't easy.

It may take you many years to discover the person you want to be and to leave your mark on the world. You'll have to be patient and persistent, and there's a good chance you'll stumble a few times along the way. But anything worth doing needs work. But as tough as it can get, the payoff is worth it.

Having goals can raise your self-esteem. It gives you a reason to work hard at school, sports, art, relationships, your religion, and doing what you believe is right. Working toward your own goals can help you face your fears. Imagine what Olympic champs like figure skaters Michelle Kwan and Sarah Hughes, gymnast Shannon Miller, and track star Marion Jones must have risked (physically and emotionally) as they struggled to win their medals. When she was a child, Martha Aarons, who plays the flute, practiced for hours to reach her goals. And Harry Potter artist Mary GrandPré worked as a waitress to keep food on her family's table while she was struggling to be recognized for her art.

At the beginning of this book, I invited you to dare to dream of a bright future ahead. Now you're more aware of skills, relationships, and activities you can choose to make that brighter future happen.

Throughout your life, you'll find that setting goals can be exciting and fulfilling, and that sharing them with other people can be incredibly rewarding. Together or alone, you're always a winner when you set out to achieve your dreams. (Of course, as you grow and change, your goals may also grow and change, which can be exciting, too!)

Although you won't be able to control everything in your future (no one can), an I CAN girl is more likely to have a fulfilled, happy, and successful life.

Want to Know More?

As you continue to strive to become the person that you want to be, here are some additional books and resources that you might want to check out for more on self-esteem, building confi- dence, coping with life, careers and leadership, and having fun:

Brave New Girls: Creative Ideas to Help Girls Be Confident, Healthy, and Happy by Joan Jacobs Brumberg (Minneapolis: Fairview Press, 1997). This book offers a lot of ideas for feeling good about yourself. From taking care of your own body to helping others, find great practical advice, tips, and activities.

Competitions: Maximizing Your Abilities by Frances A. Karnes and Tracy L. Riley (Waco, TX: Prufrock Press, 1999). This book is a treasure trove of information on selecting, entering, and competing in national contests. Featuring a list of more than 275 competitions in classical literature, general science, mathematics, and art, this book offers students a listing of national competitions in almost any talent area.

Cool Women, Hot Jobs . . . and how you can go for it, too! by Tina Schwager and Michele Schuerger (Minneapolis: Free Spirit Publishing, 2002). Nineteen women and three musical sisters (the Ahn Trio) tell about their work, how they got started, what they do, and why they love it. Each first-person story encourages you to dream big about your own future, because anything is possible.

The Girls' Guide to Life: How to Take Charge of the Issues That Affect You by Catherine Dee (Boston: Little, Brown and Company, 1997). This book is full of advice on family, school, popularity, self-esteem, body issues, and more. Full of tips, stories, and suggestions, this is a book you'll turn to again and again.

Girls Know Best: Advice for Girls from Girls on Just About Everything! compiled by Michelle Roehm (Hillsboro, OR: Beyond Words Publishing, 1997). Find helpful advice from other girls on a variety of topics that include sports, siblings, drug prevention, diversity, depression, and many more. The book also provides volunteer opportunities, ideas for strengthening your interests and skills, and ways to simply have a good time.

Girls Who Rocked the World: Heroines from Sacagawea to Sheryl Swoopes by Amelie Welden (Hillsboro, OR: Beyond Words Publishing, 1998). This book documents the true stories of thirty-three girls who accomplished extraordinary things before the age of twenty. Find yourself inspired by the young feats of Cleopatra, Helen Keller, Anne Frank, and many more.

Gutsy Girls: Young Women Who Dare by Tina Schwager and Michele Schuerger (Minneapolis: Free Spirit Publishing, 1999). In inspiring, first-person stories, twenty-five young women ages fourteen to twenty-four tell of their daring feats, from extreme sports to history-making achievements, and share the details about the sweat, persistence, and courage it takes to reach these kinds of goals.

Club Girl Tech

www.girltech.com

Find great games and inspiring stories at this site for girls. Read about girls and women using their smarts to make a difference in the world. The site also offers information on issues girls and women face, reviews of music, books, and movies, and links to other informative sites.

dgArts Online Magazine

www.dgarts.com

This Web site is the online home of *Dream/Girl* Magazine, a publication for girls that highlights interesting information about literature and the arts. Find contests, interviews with authors and artists, samples of work from girls just like you, and more.

Girl Power!

www.girlpower.gov

This site offers great information for staying healthy, mentally and physically. You'll get the scoop on science and technology careers, find challenging games and puzzles, and discover what other girls are saying about the issues that you face every day.

A Girl's World Online Clubhouse

www.agirlsworld.com

Here you'll discover a wide variety of fun things to see and do including book reviews, career information, school tips, games, projects, movies, and more. Also find contests, classes, pen pals, and opportunities for you to make a difference.

Camp Fire USA

4601 Madison Avenue
Kansas City, MO 64112
(816) 756-1950
www.campfire.org

This organization offers educational programs in hundreds of communities across the United States. Contact them for more information about programs in youth leadership, environmental education, childcare, and more.

Girl Scouts of the USA

420 Fifth Avenue
New York, NY 10018
1-800-478-7248
www.girlscouts.org

The Girl Scouts is a great way to get involved in the community while taking care of yourself and developing your interests and skills. Visit their Web site to discover new places and people, share your thoughts creatively with other girls, and search for a troop near you.

Girls Incorporated

120 Wall Street
New York, NY 10005
1-800-374-4475
www.girlsinc.org

This national organization can help you reach your full potential. Contact them for information about programs that address math and science education, positive health choices and body image, media literacy, and much more. Log on to their Web site for profiles of strong, smart, and bold girls that will inspire you to be your best.

YWCA of the USA
1015 18th Street NW, Suite 1100
Washington, DC 20036
1-800-992-2871
www.ywca.org
Contact the YWCA for a wide range of programs and services designed to enrich and transform your life. With local chapters all over the country and thousands of volunteers, this is a great resource for education, career, and volunteer opportunities.

Mentoring

The Girl Pages: A Handbook of Resources for Growing Strong, Confident, Creative Girls by Charlotte Milholland (New York: Hyperion, 1999). This resource is filled with opportunities to develop interests and skills. A listing of books, Web sites, organizations, and more make it easy to find the right opportunity for developing your leadership, civic, and other skills.

The Person Who Changed My Life: Prominent Americans Recall Their Mentors edited by Matilda Raffa Cuomo (Secaucus, NJ: Carol Publishing Group, 1999). A collection of essays from influential people who have benefited from mentor experiences, this book details how mentoring can positively change your life. Contributors include Hillary Rodham Clinton, Julia Child, Gloria Estefan, and many others.

Boys & Girls Clubs of America
www.bgca.org
This organization offers national programs that help young people develop the skills they need to succeed in life. Visit their Web site to find mentoring opportunities in health; the environment; the arts; alcohol, drug, and pregnancy prevention; leadership development; and more.

America's Promise—Alliance for Youth
909 North Washington Street, Suite 400
Alexandria, VA 22314
1-888-559-6884
www.americaspromise.org
This alliance of nearly 500 national organizations provides youth programs around the country designed to create ongoing relationships between youth and the adults in their lives—parents, mentors, tutors, or coaches. Contact them for opportunities in your area.

MENTOR/ National Mentoring Partnership
1600 Duke Street, Suite 300
Alexandria, VA 22314
(703) 224-2200
www.mentoring.org
For more than a decade, this organization has been a leader in the effort to connect America's young people with caring adult mentors. Contact them to learn about the many opportunities available in your own community.

Skills USA–VICA (Vocational Industrial Clubs of America)
P.O. Box 3000
Leesburg, VA 20177
(703) 777-8810
www.skillsusa.org
This organization is dedicated to helping students interested in trade, health, industrial, and technical careers. Contact them for more information about career

and mentoring opportunities that will help you develop your leadership, communication, and other skills.

Volunteering

The Kid's Guide to Service Projects: Over 500 Service Ideas for Young People Who Want to Make a Difference by Barbara A. Lewis (Minneapolis: Free Spirit Publishing, 1995). This book will help you address and solve problems, big and small, in your own community. You'll find step-by-step instructions for creating proclamations, press releases, surveys, and more.

The Kid's Guide to Social Action: How to Solve the Social Problems You Choose—and Turn Creative Thinking into Positive Action by Barbara A. Lewis (Minneapolis: Free Spirit Publishing, 1998). Are there problems in your school or community that need to be addressed? This step-by-step guide will help you to solve them. Learn how to write letters, make speeches, take surveys, raise funds, and more.

Action Without Borders
www.idealist.org/kt
This is a great resource for exploring the world around you and gaining inspiration to make a difference. Read up on global issues, find out about kids doing extraordinary things, discover volunteering opportunities, and find out how to turn your service ideas into action.

Do Something
www.dosomething.org
A nationwide network of young people solving problems in their communities and taking action in the world, this organization's Web site offers background information on important issues—like child abuse, racism, the environment, AIDS, and many more—and lets you know how you can help.

National Youth Leadership Council
1667 Snelling Avenue North
St. Paul, MN 55108
(651) 631-3672
www.nylc.org
This organization offers service-learning projects for young people in their individual communities and schools. Contact them to find out how you can make a difference in the lives of others while developing your own skills in leadership and civics.

Youth Service America
1101 15th Street NW, Suite 200
Washington, DC 20005
(202) 296-2992
www.ysa.org
A one-stop resource center for discovering local, national, and global volunteer opportunities, this alliance of organizations is dedicated to healthy communities and youth development in citizenship and service. Offering many services, Youth Service America can help you find the perfect volunteer opportunity for you.

Digging Deeper

In this section, you'll find some questions for teachers, parents, grandparents, relatives, fellow learners, counselors . . . and you! The questions don't have right or wrong answers. They're just meant to give you, your reading partners, and the adults you share this book with some extra ideas to talk about.

Chapter 1
Dare to Dream

1. What do you imagine your life will be like in twenty years? What family members and friends will you be sharing it with? What jobs will you and they have? Where will you live and in what kind of home?

2. Would you like to be famous for doing something special? Do you think any of your friends will become famous? Is it important to you that you or someone you know becomes well-known?

3. How did you do on the quiz on pages 5–7? Were you surprised at how well you did, or were you disappointed in your score? Why?

4. Do you think you're an I CAN girl sometimes or most of the time? Do you know any other girls who are I CAN girls? What makes them I CAN girls?

5. Were you surprised that Nydia Velázquez and Shelley Berkley, who came from poor families, became congresswomen? Why or why not? Do you think it's easier or harder to become successful if your parents don't have a lot of money?

Chapter 2
Exercising Your Self-Esteem Muscles

1. How do you feel about yourself? Do you think your self-esteem is good, average, or not very good? What makes you think so?

2. Do you ever feel that you're too hard on yourself? What can you do when this happens to feel better about yourself?

3. Are you sometimes a perfectionist? Do you know other kids who are? What do you imagine a perfect person would be like? Do you think this is a realistic goal?

4. Would you say your self-esteem depends on having boyfriends or

being popular? Do you think it will when you get older? What do you tell yourself to feel better when you're lonely?

5. Can you tell the difference between when someone's being mean to you and when you're being oversensitive? Think of a time when you were really hurt by someone's words but the other person was only kidding and didn't mean to hurt your feelings. How else could you have handled that situation?

6. Have you ever thought about how you can make the world a better place when you're older? Have you done anything to make the world a better place already? What could we do together to make the world a better place?

Chapter 3
Feel Smart by Releasing Your Brainpower

1. Do you like to read? Does reading help you feel smart? Might you feel even smarter if you read more? Why do you think you either do or don't like to read?

2. Would it be fun to join a book club, where you read and discuss books? Which of this book's ideas about reading could you use in a book club?

3. Are there kids in your class who seem smart because they like reading? Are there others who may be smart but aren't good readers?

4. Do you think that, as a rule, girls or boys are better at math? How about science? Are math and science easy or hard for you? Do you like these subjects? Are there any ideas in this book about math and science that you'd like to try for fun? Which ones?

5. Do you like to write? Do you keep a diary or journal? Do you ever write stories for fun? Have you ever sent a poem or story to a magazine or newspaper? What might it feel like to have something that you wrote published?

6. In what way(s) do you think you're creative? What are your main strengths or talents? When you have a good idea, do you finish what you start, or do you sometimes get stuck in the middle and not finish? Why do you think this happens?

7. What do you think the expression "play to your strengths" means? If you have (or if you had) a learning disability, how could you apply that idea? How could you help someone with a disability feel better about herself?

8. Have you ever had a special teacher who helped you to be your best? How did she do it? Did you especially like her? Why or why not?

Chapter 4
Improving Your Social Smarts

1. Do you feel pretty smart when it comes to getting along with others? Why or why not?

2. What traits do you look for in a close friend? Do you wish you were more popular or do you feel okay with the friends you have now?

3. In general, do you think you're kind? Do you wish you could be kinder sometimes? What could you do to become kinder?

4. Do any of the kids in your school frighten you? If so, what could you do about that? What would you do if you heard that somebody was planning to hurt you or someone else? Are there people you'd feel safe turning to? Who are they?

5. Are you happy doing things on your own sometimes? What kinds of things, if any, do you like to do by yourself? Do you ever feel lonely? What do you do at these times?

6. Do you ever do things you'd rather not do just because other people want you to? When? What might you do instead?

7. Do you think of yourself as shy or outgoing? What makes you feel more or less shy?

8. Do you think of yourself as a take-charge leader, a behind-the-scenes leader, or a follower? What types of projects would you be most comfortable taking charge of?

Chapter 5
Tuning in to Your Talents

1. What are some of the activities you really love? Are there any that you used to love but are now bored with? If so, why? Is it because the activity is harder than it once was, because other kids are better at it than you, or because it isn't as interesting as it was in the beginning?

2. Are you involved in too many activities, too few, or just the right number? What makes you think so?

3. Are you involved in both all-girl and girl-boy activities? Do you prefer one kind over the other? If so, which? Why?

4. Is it hard for you to lose? If so, what advice can you give yourself that might make losing less of a big deal?

5. Think of a time when you hit a wall trying to master a new skill. How did you handle it? What were you proud of? What do you wish you had done differently?

6. How do you feel when you see others cheating? Think of a time when you were tempted to cheat. How would you have been cheating others in that situation? How would you have cheated yourself?

Chapter 6
Exploring the World

1. What's the farthest you've ever traveled from where you live now? What do you remember most about any traveling you've done?

2. Have you ever traveled alone or in a group without your family? If so,

what did you learn from the experience? If not, do you think this would be fun or scary?

3. Do you have any pen pals or Internet pals who live far away? In what ways do their lives sound different from yours? In what ways do they sound the same?

4. Imagine that your family was going to host a foreign student in your home or that you were asked to put together a brochure about your area. What would you recommend that out-of-town visitors see?

5. What parts of the world would you like to see? What appeals to you about each one? What could you do now to help you get there someday?

Chapter 7
When Things Change

1. In general, do you think of yourself as someone who likes change or who runs from it? Why?

2. What are some big changes you've gone through in your life? How did they make you feel? Looking back, did these changes wind up being for the better or not?

3. Have you ever moved? If so, what was hard for you about it and what was easy? What helped you most as you were trying to adjust?

4. Imagine a friend confiding in you after something bad happens in her family. What might you say to comfort her? What words of advice would you give to help her get through this hard time? Are these things you can tell yourself when you're going through a hard time?

5. How easy or how hard is it for you to look at the bright side of bad things? What might help you put a positive spin on bad things when they happen to you?

Chapter 8
My Role Model, My Mentor

1. Think of adults (in real life, on television, in the movies, and in books) who you want to be like when you're older. What do you admire about them? Now think of some who you don't want to be like. What do you dislike about them?

2. Do you have more role models or more mentors in your life? What makes you think so?

3. In what areas of your life do you feel you could use a mentor? Why?

4. In what ways do you think you could be a good mentor to somebody else (for example, a younger child)? Would you like to be one? Why or why not?

5. Have you changed because of things that someone close to you has done or said? If so, what were you like before and how did the person's words or actions lead to a change?

Chapter 9
All in the Family

1. When you're curious about something, who in your family are you most likely to turn to for answers?

2. Do you ever find it hard to talk to the adults in your home? Why or why not? What would make it easier for you to talk to them? What do you do when you don't feel like telling them what's on your mind?

3. What things about your family are you most proud of? Are you ever embarrassed by anything about them? If so, when and why? What might help you stop feeling this way?

4. If you have brothers or sisters, how well do you get along with them? Are you usually mean or nice to each other? Are you ever jealous of them? What could you do to make your relationship with them better than it is? If you don't have brothers or sisters, are you ever jealous of kids that do?

5. Do you ever purposely avoid doing things your relatives are good at? If so, is that because you're afraid you won't do as well? What other reasons might there be?

Index

About the Author

Dr. Sylvia Rimm is the best-selling author of *See Jane Win* and *How Jane Won*. She is also the director of the Family Achievement Clinic in Cleveland, and a clinical professor at Case Western Reserve University School of Medicine. The host of *Family Talk with Sylvia Rimm* on public radio and author of a syndicated newspaper column on parenting, she has appeared in *Redbook* and *People* magazines and on *Oprah, 20/20,* and NBC's *Today* show. Her other books include *Why Bright Kids Get Poor Grades* and *How to Parent So Children Will Learn.*

When she's not working, she enjoys bicycling, hiking, and most importantly, spending time with her four children and nine grandchildren, who call her the "sunset grandmom" because she likes to stop whatever she's doing, wherever she is, to watch the sunset.

Other Great Books from Free Spirit

Cool Women, Hot Jobs

. . . and how you can go for it, too!

by Tina Schwager, P.T.A., A.T.,C., and Michele Schuerger

Women's career options used to be limited, but not anymore. Meet 22 women—including a fighter pilot, an Imagineer with the Walt Disney Company, and a trio of classical musicians who've shared their personal experiences and sound advice. This inspiring book is filled with ideas, information, activities, and journaling exercises readers can use to plan and pursue their dreams of an exciting and meaningful future. For ages 11 & up.

$15.95; 288 pp.; softcover; B&W photos; 6" x 9"

What Do You Really Want?

How to Set a Goal and Go for It! A Guide for Teens

by Beverly K. Bachel

This book is a step-by-step guide to goal setting, written especially for teens. Each chapter includes fun, creative exercises, practical tips, words of wisdom from famous "goal-getters," real-life examples from teens, and success stories. Includes reproducibles. For ages 11 & up.

$12.95; 144 pp.; softcover; illus.; 6" x 9"

The Right Moves to Getting Fit and Feeling Great!

by Tina Schwager, P.T.A., A.T.,C., and Michele Schuerger

This upbeat guide encourages girls to realize their full potential by developing a healthy self-image, eating right, and becoming physically fit. The pages are filled with ideas to help girls set goals, handle puberty, and pamper themselves. Includes quizzes, quotes, facts, and fun activities to guide readers down the path to becoming totally fit inside and out.

For ages 11 & up.

$15.95; 280 pp.; softcover; illus.; 7" x 9"

You're Smarter Than You Think

A Kid's Guide to Multiple Intelligences

by Thomas Armstrong, Ph.D.

In clear, simple language, this book explains the eight intelligences. Kids will learn how they can use each intelligence in school and at home, and also draw on them to plan for the future. Resources point the way to books, software, games, and organizations that help kids develop their intelligences. This timely book is recommended for all kids, their parents, and educators. For ages 8–12.

$15.95; 192 pp.; softcover; illus.; 7" x 9"

To place an order or to request a free catalog of SELF-HELP FOR KIDS® and SELF-HELP FOR TEENS® materials, please write, call, email, or visit our Web site:

Free Spirit Publishing Inc.
217 Fifth Avenue North • Suite 200 • Minneapolis, MN 55401-1299
toll-free 800.735.7323 • local 612.338.2068 • fax 612.337.5050
help4kids@freespirit.com • www.freespirit.com

Visit us on the Web!
www.freespirit.com

Stop by anytime to find our Parents' Choice Approved catalog with fast, easy, secure 24-hour online ordering; "Ask Our Authors," where visitors ask questions—and authors give answers—on topics important to children, teens, parents, teachers, and others who care about kids; links to other Web sites we know and recommend; fun stuff for everyone, including quick tips and strategies from our books; and much more! Plus our site is completely searchable so you can find what you need in a hurry. Stop in and let us know what you think!

Just point and click!

new! Get the first look at our books, catch the latest news from Free Spirit, and check out our site's newest features.

contact Do you have a question for us or for one of our authors? Send us an email. Whenever possible, you'll receive a response within 48 hours.

order! Order in confidence! Our secure server uses the most sophisticated online ordering technology available. And ordering online is just one of the ways to purchase our books: you can also order by phone, fax, or regular mail. No matter which method you choose, excellent service is our ultimate goal.

For a fast and easy way to receive our practical tips, helpful information, and special offers, send your email address to e-news@freespirit.com. View a sample letter and our privacy policy at *www.freespirit.com*.

1.800.735.7323 • fax 612.337.5050 • help4kids@freespirit.com